Smart Moves

in Six Minutes

LESSONS IN LEADERSHIP

from

AskSamDeep.com

My best to you!
Sam

Other Books by Sam Deep

Lost and Found: How One Man Found Leadership Where He Wasn't Even Looking
(with Lyle Sussman and Alex Stiber)

Act on It! Solving 101 of the Toughest Management Challenges
(with Lyle Sussman)

Close the Deal: Smart Moves for Selling
(with Lyle Sussman)

Power Tools: 33 Management Inventions You Can Use Today
(with Lyle Sussman)

Smart Moves for People in Charge: 130 Checklists to Help You Be a Better Leader
(with Lyle Sussman)

Yes, You Can! 1,200 Inspiring Ideas for Work, Home, and Happiness
(with Lyle Sussman)

What to Say to Get What You Want: Strong Words for 44 Challenging Bosses, Employees, Coworkers, and Customers
(with Lyle Sussman)

What to Ask When You Don't Know What to Say: 555 Powerful Questions to Use for Getting Your Way at Work
(with Lyle Sussman)

Smart Moves: 140 Checklists to Bring Out the Best from You and Your Team
(with Lyle Sussman)

COMEX: The Communication Experience in Human Relations
(with Lyle Sussman)

A Program of Exercises for Management and Organizational Behavior
(with James A. Vaughan)

Introduction to Business: A Systems Approach
(with William D. Brinkloe)

Studies in Organizational Psychology
(with Bernard M. Bass)

Current Perspectives for Managing Organizations
(with Bernard M. Bass)

Copyright© 2012 Sam Deep

ISBN 978-1-4507-3064-8

Printed in the United States of America

Cover Design, Text Design, and Editing
by Higgins & Associates

Set in 10 point Adobe Trebuchet
with Park Avenue Display

Environmentally-Friendly Printing

on DOMTAR EarthChoice®
High-quality paper with a conscience

This book is available at special discounts for bulk purchases in the U.S. by corporations, institutions, and other organizations. For more information, please contact Sam Deep at (412) 487-2379, or e-mail sam@asksamdeep.com.

About this Book

My friend Marcus Fish conceived this resource at our lunch at Panera in Wexford, PA in the early months of 2009. Later, we built the vehicle that houses the leadership email blasts that hundreds of executives read each week at AskSamDeep.com.

The idea for the web site was to create something found nowhere else. Subscribers have a place they can turn to for concrete, no-nonsense solutions to the leadership dilemmas of the new millennium. Each week on Wednesday morning those subscribers receive a new question (e.g., "Why am I here?") along with a one-minute answer. If their curiosity is sufficiently piqued, they click on a link to a fuller, five-minute answer. In this book all six minutes of answers come to you at once.

On the following pages we bring the best from the archives on the site to you and your colleagues in a readily accessible format. In addition, each one of the 27 issues in the Contents has been updated, strengthened, and sharpened to achieve its own unique focus.

You'll also benefit from cross-referencing found throughout the text. Whenever there's material elsewhere in the book supporting an insight you're studying, page references to that material appear. For example, when it will help you to know more about using questions for impact, you'll be led to that resource by the page reference (43-45).

Breakthrough!

Please do not use the advice in this book to become more knowledgeable about leadership. These insights are not for your head. Rather, they are meant for your hands, mouth, and feet. We want you to convert the information into action.

To this end, each ASK closes with the section, *Breakthrough!* There you learn how to transform what you read into concrete steps that will delight you, engage your people, and fortify your organization.

Acknowledgements

Thank you...

Professor Pete "Granny" Smith for lighting my writing fires in freshman English

Bernie Bass who gave me my first authorship opportunity as his sidekick on *Current Perspectives for Managing Organizations*

Those wonderful people to work with (aka clients) whose needs for solutions helped me to grow and to develop the ideas on leadership that you're about to read

Marcus Fish whose suggestion it was to create the original leadership email blasts as well as asksamdeep.com

Colleen Higgins, my editor, whose deft talent helped to transform web site speak into suitable book prose

...and, of course, **Dianne** who has been always encouraging, always supportive, and always loving

CONTENTS

Smart Moves

in Six Minutes

27 LESSONS IN LEADERSHIP

from

AskSamDeep.com

To lead the people, walk behind them.

~Lao Tzu

What is servant leadership?

One-Minute Answer: In two different Gospel books of the New Testament, Jesus of Nazareth gave His followers the same leadership lesson. In Mark 10:42-44 it's reported this way:

> Jesus called them together and said, "You know that those who are regarded as rulers of the Gentiles lord it over them, and their high officials exercise authority over them. Not so with you. Instead, whoever wants to become great among you must be your servant, and whoever wants to be first must be slave of all." (NIV)

This counsel from the most influential leader who ever lived spawned a revolutionary philosophy of influence. Books have been written about it, workshops have been conducted on it, and institutes have been established to further it. The notion of servant leadership has caused executives, supervisors, and even parents to rethink the way they exercise authority.

So what's it all about and why is this leadership style such a good thing? After all, the notion of servanthood carries a distinctly negative connotation in the brave new world of the 21st Century.

Even advocates of the idea seek to rename it. A former client of mine tried "leadership through service". But this euphemism entirely misses the point, which is that leaders are to sacrifice their needs in favor of the needs of followers in order to win their hearts. At the close of the workday, servant leaders do not wonder "What did my people do for me today?" but rather "What did I do for my people?"

Five-Minute Answer: Servant leadership inspires people to follow you. Jesus declared that becoming subservient makes that happen. Here's what leaders who fulfill his prescription do:

1. **Display exemplary behavior.** When I taught leadership to second year MBA's I would ask, "Why is it important to do the right thing?" It was discouraging to rarely hear the answer, "Because it's the right thing to do." This question anchored a module on business ethics, but goes beyond that issue. Doing the right thing also means showing to followers in your behavior the very

behavior you expect from them. For example, are you as honest with them as you insist that they be with you?

2. **Listen to them and to their ideas.** A major complaint children have of parents is, "They don't listen to me." Children and employees, alike, feel undervalued and invalidated by a leader who is not interested in their thoughts. (39-41)

3. **Learn and meet their expectations.** In that same MBA course another revealing question was, "What would happen if you asked your direct reports what they need from you as a leader to help them succeed?" Not a popular question! A typical response was, "That would be a sign of weakness! You're the leader, and you should know how to supervise them." A question for you: How would you feel if your boss asked for your expectations with a genuine intent of fulfilling them? An executive once answered, "I'd think I'd died and gone to heaven."

4. **Keep them informed.** "No one tells you anything around here!" Sound familiar? Don't let that be the mantra where you lead. The scarcest resource in any workplace is good information. Most bad decisions can be traced to bad or missing data. Your job is to keep your people equipped with the most timely, abundant, and accurate information on the planet.

5. **Manage by wandering around.** Author and speaker Tom Peters says it is more important for leaders to be visible than to be on planes, in meetings, or poring over paperwork. His idea of MBWA enables you to show an interest in people and their work, lets you reveal your human side, gives you occasion to encourage them, affords the chance to ask them questions, and may even give your employees an opening to teach you something.

6. **Involve them in decisions that affect them.** Express your desire to let others influence their future. "I've been asked to _____. What should I be looking at as I make that decision?" "What do you see as the advantages and disadvantages of_____?" "I'm preparing to _____. What might I be missing in taking that action?"

7. **Give them more important work to do.** Make others feel and be more important in these ways: Trust someone with a decision you once made. ("What should we do?") Turn over a complete

operation to someone. ("You're in charge.") Send someone to a meeting to represent you. ("Speak for us.") These strategies might also help you get out of the weeds you're stuck in and elevate you to a more strategic role—where you belong!

8. **Keep getting smaller so they can get bigger.** In his book *Good to Great*, Jim Collins identifies Level Five leadership as the pinnacle of executive capability. He defines it as a paradoxical blend of personal humility and professional will. The word humility signifies a lowliness and submissiveness that diminishes you as it elevates people around you. For many, this prescription is the hardest part of servant leadership to swallow, but it is also the most transformational. You'll know you've made it when those at succeeding hierarchical levels call you a "real person".

9. **Help them grow.** In a major way, #7 and #8 above cause people to grow. Another key source of development on the job is training, coaching, and mentoring. Test yourself on these dimensions of employee growth with your answer to this question: "Are my people significantly more valuable to their team, to other teams, to customers, to themselves, and to me than they were a year ago?" (75-77)

10. **Be their champion.** Provide all the resources your people need to perform at the highest levels. Represent their interests to higher ups. Go to bat for them; defend them; protect them. Showcase them to other decision makers who may be in a position to advance their careers.

11. **Praise them.** William James once said, "The deepest craving in human nature is the desire to be appreciated." You'll serve the people you influence by recognizing this need and meeting it. A simple "Thank you" is often all it takes. (55-57)

12. **Treat them with dignity.** Remember their names and important things about them. Act as though "rank has no privilege" by not sticking your executive perks in their faces. Treat their families with respect at every opportunity. Promote from within when you can. Pay them competitive wages.

Breakthrough! Which of these servant leader behaviors will your people begin seeing more of *tomorrow?*

The price of greatness is responsibility.

~Winston Churchill

What are some of the most inspiring thoughts about leadership?

One-Minute Answer: You and I wouldn't define leadership the same way. That may be one reason why the two of us think we see so little of it—whether in business, government, or not-for-profit enterprise. What others practice as supposed leadership is not what we "know" it to be. So who's right? Let's turn to the great thoughts of experts and proven leaders to discover from their eyes what leadership looks like.

Five-Minute Answer: Here are some great quotes about leadership. I've taken the liberty to attach to each one meaning that adds to our understanding of this incredibly essential yet elusive pursuit.

1. **"The pilot of a ship is worth as much as all the crew."**
    ~Philo Judaeus

    These 2000-year-old words from the Alexandrian philosopher speak to the central role that leadership plays. When I check into a hotel, walk into a store, or sit down in a restaurant I can gauge within minutes the quality of leadership there. So can you! And I never leave a good (or bad) service experience thinking "good (or bad) *employees.*" No, I look back and think "good (or bad) *leadership.*" Philo was right on!

2. **"Leadership is liberating people to do what is required of them."**
    ~Max Depree

    My all-time favorite definition of leadership! You gotta love a sentence with the words "liberating" and "required" so close together. Leaders "liberate" by removing the roadblocks their people face. Do you?

3. **"When the elephants fight, it's the grass that suffers."**
    ~African proverb

    Very few team leaders get along well when their teams don't; very few teams collaborate as their leaders fight. This is Philo's point remade.

4. "Those who are in the highest places, and have the most power, have the least liberty, because they are the most observed."   ~John Tillotson

   When you supervise, you live in a fishbowl. The people you hope to influence watch everything you do. You cannot be a negative role model. You must not declare, "Do as I say, not as I do."

5. "We'll start the war right here!"

                         ~Brigadier General Teddy Roosevelt, Jr.

   When his D-Day troops landed on the wrong spot on Utah Beach, the son of a Rough Rider didn't wait for new orders. He showed can-do, individual initiative unimaginable in the German ranks. Are you prepared to seek forgiveness, rather than permission, when it's the right thing to do?

6. "For if the trumpet give an uncertain sound, who shall prepare himself to the battle?"   ~1 Corinthians 14:8

   Your people look to you for direction, and while your decisions must be measured and thoughtful, you can't be hesitant or wishy-washy. Such decisiveness is particularly important in times of challenge when people need certainty and stability.

7. "All of the great leaders have had one characteristic in common: it was the willingness to confront unequivocally the major anxiety of the people in their time. This, and not much else is the essence of leadership."   ~John Kenneth Galbraith

   Yes! Your people need to know that you understand and feel their pain. Even more, they look to you to ease it.

8. "In any series of elements to be controlled, a selected small fraction, in terms of numbers of elements, always accounts for a large fraction in terms of effect."   ~Vilfredo Pareto

   Immeasurably valuable words! Pareto's 80/20 Rule says that 80% of our business comes from 20% of our marketing, 20% of our customers consume 80% of our time, and 20% of our employees do 80% of the work. Its significance for your leadership is this: with 20% of your effort, or in 20% of your workday, you add 80% of your value. Figure out (ask others?) what that 20% is and do more of it.

9. "A man is rich in proportion to the number of things which he can afford to let alone."   ~Henry David Thoreau

The "richest" leaders have found their 20% by delegating responsibilities that shouldn't consume their day. They have been liberated for strategic thinking in exchange for tactical implementation they can trust to others.

10. **"If you want a place in the sun you've got to expect a few blisters."**   ~*Abigail Van Buren*
    I saw a statistic that 55% of all teachers would agree to fire their School Superintendent. The vote of no confidence among your followers may never get that bad, but you'll always have your detractors. This was one of the reasons President Harry Truman said, "If you can't stand the heat, get out of the kitchen."

11. **"As long as you can stand up, you keep going."**
                                          ~*1st Sergeant Leonard Lomell*
    Shot in the side as he stepped onto the beach at Normandy, Ranger Lomell continued to direct his men to their objective at Point du Hoc in France. Do you keep going when "wounded" as an inspiration to your team?

12. **"You can't lead a cavalry charge if you think you look funny on a horse."**   ~*John Peers*
    If you are uncertain about your impact as a leader, the contents of this book will help to dissolve any lack of self-confidence.

13. **"If your actions inspire others to dream more, learn more, do more and become more, you are a leader."**
                                          ~*John Quincy Adams*
    Adams' focus on public servants' growth and development is equally instrumental for corporate leaders.

14. **"My own definition of leadership is this: The capacity and the will to rally men and women to a common purpose and the character that inspires confidence."**
                                          ~*General Bernard Montgomery*
    "Monty" adds two essential leadership ingredients to this list. First, leaders excel when they help people discover a sense of purpose and meaning in their work. Second, followers look for integrity, more than anything else, in their leaders.

Breakthrough! Which of these aphorisms calls to you? Do you struggle with a challenge that this philosophy can resolve for you?

The greatest mistake a man can make is to be afraid of making one.

~Elbert Hubbard

What is the biggest mistake that leaders make?

One-Minute Answer: One morning not long ago I enjoyed a grande half-caff with four shots of mocha syrup at Starbucks with my Pennsylvania State Representative. We had a pleasant time getting acquainted. As often happens when a new friend learns of my passion for leadership, the conversation turned into Q&A. In this case he asked the most important question of all—the one above.

You might ask, "Why is a *negative* question at the top of your list? Isn't it always better to ask a positive one?" No! We learn more in the negative than in the positive. Our failures teach us far more than our victories do.

Look at it this way. When I educate managers on the best practices of leadership, they appear to have an easy time reassuring themselves that they follow many of them. By contrast, when I identify leadership behaviors to *avoid* I encounter greater candor and even halting introspection as those same managers wonder, "Do I resemble that?" In other words, negative teaching convicts more convincingly than positive teaching does.

If you are willing to confront your leadership demons, prepare yourself to run into the most serious faults residing in the managers I find myself privileged to coach.

Five-Minute Answer: When my Representative asked the question, I suggested that there was more than one major roadblock to leadership success, but I had only enough time to elaborate on the first two. (Hopefully, he's reading this and will benefit from adding the other nine.)

1. **Succumbing to fear.** Leaders who second-guess themselves create indecision among their reports. Those who look over their shoulders to see if anyone is approaching with a hidden dagger, take their eye off the prize. Those who request permission from higher ups rather than seek forgiveness, when necessary, limit progress. Insecure leaders often fall somewhere on a scale running from "wimp" on one end to "bully" on the other. Get off that scale!

2. **Failing to hold people accountable.** If you don't establish your rules of the road and if you don't impose consequences for failure to obey them, you'll lose the respect of your best people. If you ignore or accommodate non-performers and troublemakers, you deserve the poor results you get.

3. **Refusing to learn.** When is the last time you were able to say, "I was wrong?" If you believe you seldom make mistakes, if other's criticism of you is rarely valid, and if you believe you know more than the people around you, people are suffering from your insufferability. And neither are you getting any better.

4. **Not seeing themselves as others do.** Soon after becoming a leadership coach I recognized the most important service I provide. That is to help leaders recognize the three "you's": (1) the "you" that they see, (2) the "you" that others around them see, and (3) the "you" that is. And of these three, the second is the one that counts. It determines the impact you're having on others and therefore the degree of good or bad you contribute to *their* contribution. Leaders who are unaware of their impact or, worse yet, don't care about it are off the rolls of inspiring leaders.

5. **Relating to people as objects.** Do you connect with the people you lead out of their roles—"admin", "technician", "vice president"—or as individual human beings with feelings, pain, wishes, ambitions, weaknesses, and desires for love and acceptance? If you're having more luck getting people to use their hands than their hearts, you'll profit from bringing more compassion into your relationships with those who look up to you.

6. **Not delegating enough.** Are you doing work that your company ought to be paying less to have done? Are your dives down to the tactical altitude of three feet keeping you from being fully operational at the strategic altitude of 30,000 feet? Does the time you spend in the weeds get in your people's way and suppress their growth?

7. **Burying their heads in the sand.** Do you shy away from confrontation? Do you avoid bad news? Do you sweep interpersonal conflict under the rug? Do you act as if things are better than they are? Leaders who display an aversion to the negative encourage direct reports to protect them from depressing outcomes by misrepresenting the facts and at times

outright lying about them.

8. **Valuing "what" over "how."** Consider these exhortations of employees: "Remain focused!" "Stay the course!" "Show your commitment!" "Don't lose sight of our goals!" "Make the numbers!" If any of them sound like you, you're a *what* leader. You believe that keeping people focused on outcomes will produce them. If I was choosing a boss, I'd rather work for one who valued outcomes just as much, but coached me through the *how*; that is, helping me learn and apply the right things to do to make outcomes happen.

9. **Acting unethically.** Don't skip over this one so quickly! All leaders—just like you—believe their actions are either highly ethical or fully justified. Given what I hear from the people who report to them, that is not always a valid assumption.

10. **Leading in a spoke network.** When you sit at the hub of a spoke network, your employees communicate largely through you to others, as well as directly to you, in the discharge of their duties. If, instead, information on your team flies freely in whatever direction is needed to be optimally effective with each task, you lead in a *star* network. When your self-protective need to control the flow of messages launches a spoke network, creativity is clogged and progress is thwarted.

11. **Being failure-preventers rather than success-insurers.** Would you rather work for someone whose focus was on keeping you out of trouble or one who empowered you to become all you could be? Would you admire a boss who chided you not to make mistakes or one who spotlighted exciting goals? Would you thrive under the tutelage of a manager who first dwelt on the downside of every opportunity or one who first made an encouraging case for the benefits? Notice that failure-preventing leaders typically reside at the hub of spoke-reporting networks.

Breakthrough! Which leadership shortcoming on this list do you vow to correct?

Snowflakes are one of nature's most fragile things, but look at what they can do when they stick together.

~Vesta M. Kelly

What is a team (or family) charter?

One-Minute Answer: George Peppard starred as Colonel John "Hannibal" Smith in the '80s TV comedy-drama-spoof *The A-Team*. The inevitable line spoken by Hannibal at the close of each episode was "I love it when a plan comes together." Why did the A-Team's plan always come together? Because each person did exactly what was needed to support other team members in their roles, empowering the team to accomplish its mission.

A team charter breeds teamwork in two ways. First, it communicates and validates what members can count on receiving from each other in order to fulfill their various roles. Second, it's a benchmark against which performance feedback can be given and against which members can be held accountable for making team plans come together.

A team charter is not a job description for individual member roles (the *what*). It is rather a description of the <u>behavioral</u> expectations members have for *how* colleagues will fulfill their roles.

Five-Minute Answer: I've advised many groups in the crafting of their team charters. Here are the most popular entries on those documents. The number of items on a charter is normally between 8 and 10. Choose what makes sense for your team from this list after revising them to suit your culture and adding items unique to your situation.

1. We collectively and energetically work toward company targets that are larger than any of our individual functions.

2. We defend and look out for each other.

3. We share our ideas, opinions, and feelings openly and honestly.

4. When we have issues with each other we speak to the person affected and do not go behind that person's back to others.

5. We welcome disagreement and diversity of opinion.

6. We debate issues to resolution, and merit most likely wins.

7. We listen to each other.

8. We challenge each other's assumptions and assertions with directness, courtesy, and respect.

9. We ask each other for help and it is freely given.

10. We make the best use of the talents, skills, and strengths on the team.

11. We support team decisions once they are made.

12. We build each other up through recognition, critique, and even constructive criticism.

13. We are as eager for each other's success as we are for our own.

14. We share with each other the resources we need to do our jobs.

15. We keep each other fully informed, respecting each other's time and priorities.

16. We do a great job of fulfilling each other's needs and meeting each other's expectations. We remain fully accountable to each other.

17. We work at improving relationships within the team that are in need of nurturing, strengthening, and even healing.

18. We resolve destructive conflict that arises out of our disagreements.

Breakthrough! Six actions will help make a team charter a living, breathing document.

First, involve the team in its creation; letting members declare the behaviors central to mission accomplishment. The discussion that generates the list will be a marvelous team-building activity all by itself.

Second, have everyone on the team express their dedication by signing the final document.

Third, keep it out and visible on the walls of the rooms where the team most often meets.

Fourth, have the team leader teach a "team charter" class as part of the orientation of all new members.

Fifth, every six months have the team rate its collective adherence to the items on the charter followed by specific vows to get better on the lowest scored items.

Sixth, blend charter items into the company's performance appraisal form, or have the team leader give each member personal feedback on living the charter.

I am not looking for the best players... I'm looking for the right players.

~Coach Herb Brooks,
rebuffing criticism of his selections for the
1980 USA Olympic Gold Medal Hockey Team

How can we increase unity on our team?

One-Minute Answer: In 1979 the Pittsburgh Pirates won their last World Series. The star on that team, Willie Stargell, would eventually enter the Major League Baseball Hall of Fame. Another player, Dave Parker, also achieved some distinction as an outstanding athlete. The rest of the team consisted largely of journeymen ball players, many of whom never again had an opportunity to experience a season like this.

Unlike the case for most world champions, few Pirates were at or near the top of the statistical heap that year. Yet, the Buccos were the winningest team in the National League. According to the Baseball Almanac, "The championship title capped off a Cinderella season in which 'Pops' (Stargell) and his 'Family' brought fun back to baseball."

Pirate fans past their early 40's will forever remember the sight of the seventh inning stretch of the final game, when player wives danced on top of the Pirate dugout to the rhythms of Sister Sledge's "We are Family." It was the squad's hymn. The unity it reflected was the main ingredient in Pittsburgh's recipe for success. When asked in post-season interviews to describe how the song reflected their season, players would point to the many dimensions of their camaraderie. "Pops" himself summed it up as, "We put aside a lot of petty jealousies."

Does your team have differences it needs to put aside?

Five-Minute Answer: I have seen each of the tools below increase team unity. The right one for your team—or several working in combination—can yield dramatic results. But rarely is any single intervention at a single point in time enough to do the trick. Disunity can be born overnight; unity can't. Think of receiving a bad cut on your arm. It happens in an instant, but it takes a while to clean it thoroughly, disinfect it, stitch it, protect the stitches, endure the healing process, remove the stitches, and patiently wait for most—never all—of the scar to fade. Take the time to heal the wound.

1. **Knight a team leader.** Sometimes upper management lacks either the wisdom or the courage to openly and visibly authorize a clear leader of the team. As a result, in-charge wannabes forever duke it out.

2. **Knight a servant leader.** When the person at the head follows the proscriptions for servant leadership, members will experience a more unity-friendly team. (3-5)

3. **Ensure well-run meetings.** Train team leaders in the art of running effective meetings and team members in behaving productively in those meetings.

4. **Give the team a glorious cause.** Provide teams with a reason for existence beyond a mundane list of corporate goals. Make it a powerful common purpose—a desirable future, an inspiring vision, a fantastic dream. Get them excited about a picture of success they'll want to paint together.

5. **Establish a team charter.** Have members acknowledge and clarify their expectations of each other. See that they regularly evaluate how well the charter is being honored and that they take steps to make it so. (15-17)

6. **Increase intimacy among members.** Aristotle said, "People never really know each other until they have eaten a certain amount of salt together." Several of the tools on this list will serve to build relationships. There are another half-dozen exercises I'm aware of that even more directly address this need. If you're not on a salt-free diet, give me a call at (412) 487-2379 to learn about them. (59-61)

7. **Introduce the elephants in the room.** Here's a strong statement for your consideration. *Every team yet to achieve its full potential has at least one interpersonal relationship in need of healing.* Fail to uncover and confront this relationship and you'll fail to achieve team unity. (27-29)

8. **Eliminate sources of competition.** What might there be in the task assigned to the group, in the performance management system, in the culture of the organization, in the leadership of the team, or in the personality of its members that creates a destructively competitive environment? How will you replace competitiveness with cooperation? (31-33)

9. **Counsel disruptive members.** Sometimes there's a member of the team who serves as its lightning rod. That person's wake may

be battering and even sinking other boats in the harbor. Whatever the nature of that dysfunctional behavior, it must be addressed as quickly, directly, and tactfully as possible. (51-53)

10. **Terminate incorrigible members.** Once a disruptive team member has resisted every opportunity to reform, and the situation is not getting better on its own, it may be time to remove that person from the team.

11. **Add team players.** Look for a proven record of team play when you either replace team members or expand their numbers. Note that there's often an inverse relationship between people's technical excellence and their readiness to contribute to a collective effort.

12. **Increase the emotional competence of members.** Provide training and coaching to team members to increase their understanding of how their emotional fabric affects their behavior as well as their working relationships with others.

13. **Eliminate obstacles.** Try this revealing and healing exercise for your team. It begins by detailing very clearly and graphically your vision of teamwork. Next, let the team identify where they believe they stand in relationship to the vision. The greatest value comes when you have them list all the barriers they see standing in the way of realizing that vision. After you get them to single out the three or four most daunting barriers, extract vows for appropriate actions to overcome the barriers and achieve the vision.

14. **Assign a team coach.** When the health of any team is key to the success of your organization, consider embedding in that team an outside professional akin to the way that war correspondents are assigned. That person observes the team in action, gives them feedback on their effectiveness, and recommends improvements in process. While not always present, the team coach attends key meetings, provides training and facilitation as needed, and ensures good use of the tools above.

Breakthrough! Go over this list with your team. Generate a healthy debate. As a group, agree to implement two or three of these unifying strategies and follow through together.

These are scraps from the table of wisdom that if well digested, yield strong nourishment to thy mind.

~Benjamin Franklin
Poor Richard's Almanack

What are the cleverest sayings about teamwork?

One-Minute Answer: One of the most difficult client requests for me to fulfill is to stand in front of a group of employees and convince them of the benefits of teamwork. Preaching is rarely effective at changing behavior. Our words *educate* more reliably than they *rehabilitate*.

But then sometimes the words of others lend impact that I don't have on my own, particularly when they are witty, can be traced to well-known personalities, or transmit powerful images or stories.

Consider, for example, this popular factoid about geese flying in formation.

1. As each goose flaps its wings, the birds behind are literally uplifted. A "V" formation provides a flock with 71% more flying range than each bird can manage alone.

2. A goose that falls out of formation immediately feels the drag and resistance of solo flight and quickly returns to leverage the lifting power of the birds ahead.

3. A lead goose that tires rotates toward the rear of the formation and another goose takes over the point position.

4. Geese toward the rear of the formation honk to encourage those up front to maintain good speed.

5. When a goose gets sick, wounded, or shot two companions relinquish the benefits of formation to follow their distressed comrade and administer help and protection. They stand by this member of the flock until he or she flies again or dies. Eventually they resume flight on their own, with another formation, or rejoin their original flock.

These five points convict us about how we should behave in human work teams. With any luck, the phrases that follow will have a similar impact on you as well as on those who you hope to spur on to greater solidarity.

Five-Minute Answer: Use these quotes as you wish. Simply enjoy them. Post a teamwork thought for the week in your office to inspire others. Or, attribute the need for teamwork to personalities that your listeners may heed. ("Benjamin Franklin once said...")

The Necessity for Teamwork

"We must indeed all hang together, or most assuredly we shall all hang separately."   *~Benjamin Franklin*

"Sticks in a bundle are unbreakable."   *~African proverb*

"They said you have to use your five best players, but I found you win with the five that fit together best."

~Red Auerbach, Coach of the Boston Celtics

"If a house be divided against itself, that house cannot stand."

~Mark 3:25

"When the elephants fight, it's the grass that suffers."

~African proverb

[Until we collect people around us of similar mind we are vulnerable, and we aren't as useful to others as we can be.]

The Strength of Teamwork

"One man may hit the mark, another blunder; but heed not these distinctions. Only from the alliance of the one, working with and through the other, are great things born."

~Antoine de Saint-Exupéry

"Never doubt that a small group of thoughtful, committed people can change the world. Indeed, it is the only thing that ever has."

~Margaret Mead

"When a team outgrows individual performance and learns team confidence, excellence becomes a reality."   *~Joe Paterno*

"The pope and a peasant know more between them than the pope alone."   *~Italian proverb*

[Our impact is magnified exponentially when people with the same vision we have walk beside us.]

Actions Required of Teamwork

"The most important name on your shirt is the one on the front."
~*Herb Brooks, Coach of 1980 USA Olympic Gold Medal Hockey Team*

"No member of a crew is praised for the rugged individuality of his rowing."   ~*Ralph Waldo Emerson*

"You cannot sink someone else's end of the boat and still keep your own afloat."   ~*Charles Bower*

"Check your ego at the door."   ~Sign placed by Lionel Ritchie for music legends as they entered to record the song "We Are the World"

"Gettin' good players is easy. Gettin' 'em to play together is the hard part."   ~*Casey Stengel*
[As soon as we are willing to submerge our individual needs for those of the team our collective power is unleashed.]

Benefits to Team Members

"Teams share the burden and divide the grief."   ~*Doug Smith*

"Light is the task where many share the toil."   ~*Homer*

"It is one of the most beautiful compensations of this life that no man can sincerely try to help another without helping himself."
~*Ralph Waldo Emerson*

"Don't try to pull yourself up by your own bootstraps."
~*Proverb of unknown origin*

"There is great comfort and inspiration in the feeling of close human relationships and its bearing on our mutual fortunes."   ~*Walt Disney*
[Giving to others more than you take from them is freeing and strengthening, not sacrificial and weakening.]

Breakthrough! Which one of these quotes best explains the need your team has for cohesiveness? How can you use it to get people's attention and convince them to support each other more fully?

A thick skin is a gift from God.

~Konrad Adenauer

Why do people fight?

One-Minute Answer: When Benjamin Franklin opined that death and taxes were the only inevitable things in life, he was a bit short of reality. There's one more certainty in our existence—*conflict*.

There are at least three reasons for this. First, we live in a world of ever increasing complexity, stress, and diversity where the status quo is continually confronted and challenged. Second, conflict is a natural by-product of human relationships. We each bring our own unique values, beliefs, and needs to the table, and those values, beliefs, and needs are not always compatible with others. Finally, we work in a world that imposes limits. We often get less than we want; so we compete with each other to get the best we can, given the options offered and the constraints imposed.

Before I answer the question above, let me say that conflict is not always a bad thing, and is often a good thing. Without it, ideas that need to be challenged might go unchecked; troubles in the dark that are harming us might never be brought to the light of day; opportunities for creative problem solving might disappear. That may be why Thomas Jefferson said, "A little rebellion now and then is a good thing."

Five-Minute Answer: People fight for many reasons. Consider these common origins of interpersonal discord:

1. **Prejudice/bias.** Strife within organizations is sometimes traced to "personalities". This is one person agitated by another based simply on how one feels about that person. That judgement could stem from another person's habits, style, values, beliefs, appearance, race, origins, relationships with others, past behavior, and a universe of other personal qualities.

2. **Nastiness/stubbornness.** Some people go through life with a chip on their shoulder in a hunt for combatants. This predilection might arise from an unhappy life that has soured them toward the people around them. It can also be a reaction to pain that is situational or buried in the past. It may be motivated by a powerful need to be right coming from who-knows-where.

3. **Sensitivity/hurt.** This occurs when a person, because of insecurity, a history of emotional trauma, or excessive conflict in life, easily feels attacked by criticism or other interpersonal directedness. You may know people who are a ticking time bomb of emotion.

4. **Emotional/mental instability.** Several years ago a medical study reported that of all the adults in the United States who are not under any form of treatment for a behavior disorder, 18% of them should be. In other words, one in five of the people you live with and work next to could be diagnosed as emotionally disturbed or mentally ill.

5. **Differences in perception/values.** Much conflict results from the varying ways people view the world. Such incongruent views are traceable to differences in upbringing, culture, race, experience, occupation, socioeconomic class and people's faith or lack thereof.

6. **Differences over facts.** A fact is a piece of data that can be quantified or an event that can be documented. Arguments over facts need not last very long since they are verifiable. But a statement like, "It is a fact that you are insensitive to my feelings," is neither documentable nor quantifiable, and is actually a difference in perception. (See #5.)

7. **Differences over goals/priorities.** An argument about whether a hospital should be known more for the quality of its teaching, patient care, or research is a disagreement over goals. Such differences can be constructive or destructive. It's good when it triggers a healthy debate over the competing merit of each approach during a strategic planning meeting. But, such differences of opinion carried into the hospital could spell disaster. In other words, before any team begins to do its work, differences over goals and priorities must be resolved.

8. **Differences over methods.** Two sides may have similar goals, but disagree about how to achieve them. For example, what are the best practices for providing outstanding patient care? Debates resulting from differences in methods, if conducted honestly and responsibly, can be a rejuvenating tonic to a family, team, or organization.

9. **Competition for scarce resources.** Two managers might argue over who has the greatest need for an assistant, whose budget should be increased more, or how to allocate recently purchased laptop computers. In our world it is increasingly true that want exceeds wherewithal.

10. **Competition for supremacy.** This occurs when one person seeks to outdo or outshine another person in order to gain approval. You might see it when two employees compete for a promotion or for decision-making authority in your organization. Whenever I embraced one of my standard poodles, the other instantly appeared out of nowhere for the same show of affection.

11. **Unfulfilled expectations.** Many of the root causes listed above contribute to one person not fulfilling the expectations of another. Unfulfilled expectations are the ultimate cause of divorce, firings, and other forms of relational breakdown. Expectations go unmet because they are unreasonable, inappropriate, too numerous, or *unstated*—the commonest culprit.

12. **Misunderstanding.** So much of what looks at first glance like one of the eleven causes described above often turns out to be nothing more than communication breakdown. Interpersonal communication, if not attended to with care, is as likely to fail as to succeed. And when it does, a receiver's unwarranted inferences about a sender's intent often trigger interpersonal conflict. One of the best examples of this is the inaccuracy inherent in email as a medium of exchange for important ideas.

Breakthrough! In the relationship most important to you, which of the twelve causes are most often at the root of the conflict and disagreement the two of you experience? Does uncovering the cause suggest remedies? (35-37)

Sometime they'll give a war and nobody will come.

~Carl Sandburg

How can I keep fights from breaking out?

One-Minute Answer: Conflict *prevention* is much easier than conflict *resolution*. As division widens, emotions escalate, and hurts deepen, interpersonal discord becomes more resistant to treatment.

It's quite easy to keep fights from breaking out. So why don't leaders take this approach? The simplest answer is that they don't know what to do. Another reason is that they don't think strategically enough to act today to prevent an unpleasant tomorrow. Perhaps the biggest reason is that many leaders refuse to take their heads out of the sand and admit to the existence of interpersonal conflict in their midst.

Five-Minute Answer: So what can you do to minimize destructive disagreement on your team (or in your family) so that you don't have to play the role of referee?

1. **Put your team on the same directional page.** Give them a powerful purpose, a common cause, and a new tomorrow that they can get excited to work toward together. Make it clear, definitive, and engaging. Cause them to feel as they would if they were erecting a house for a family in need.

2. **Put your team on the same priorities page.** See that your team operates from a distinctive set of strategic goals. These are the transformations or improvements that they agree with you are necessary to achieve the outcomes (revenue, profits, et al.) assigned to them. They may not agree with the appropriateness of every outcome. That's understandable. But disagreement about how the team will realize those outcomes is unacceptable.

3. **Make clear who does what.** Provide team members with job descriptions that identify who's responsible for getting every part of the mission accomplished. Often the most serious ownership questions are raised between rather than within teams. Equally crucial here is not to permit responsibility to fall through the cracks: "That's not my job!"

4. **Make your needs known.** I once worked for a senior administrator who must have thought he hired Kreskin the mind reader. I knew what my duties were, but I had few clues about his values and about how he wanted me to perform my duties. Don't do to your team what he did to me. Give them your rules of the road to minimize discord with you and with each other.

5. **Hire team players.** What a novel thought! When you hire people do you make the common error of assuming that experience and education are the best predictors of success? Or do you look for evidence that the candidate in front of you works well with others and will jell with the incumbents on your team? (67-69)

6. **Assemble compatible people.** There are a number of validated assessments that can help you organize your teams so they are well-matched in the way they are hard-wired. While you don't want a staff of clones, you *do* want to head off, or at least anticipate, personality clashes.

7. **Deal with trouble makers.** Pareto's Law suggests that 20% of your employees cause 80% of the interpersonal conflict on your team. Put these 20%ers on notice. Do not tolerate fighting and bickering. Step in quickly to resolve instances of conflict. Impose consequences when necessary. Set an example, and make one if you need to.

8. **Get help for those who need it.** It may be that a "lightning rod" on your team is a soul in need of professional counsel.

9. **Create a team charter.** Establish clear rules of the road to guide employee behavior. Get team members to agree to treat each other with manners, civility, and thoughtfulness. (15-17; 71-73)

10. **Insist on great internal customer service.** So many executives demand exceptional service for ultimate customers and pay too little attention to disarray among the internal functions that must harmonize in order for such service to occur. Require nothing less than close inter-team collaboration. Evaluate it in your performance review system. (63-65; 87-97)

11. **Distribute resources fairly.** Take great care to allocate people, equipment, material, facilities, and credit for accomplishments so rationally that employees are disinclined to compete for these assets. Not sure how well you do this? Ask your people!

12. **Eliminate "Who did it?"** When problems occur, look for solutions rather than places to blame. Set a standard on your team for problem solving rather than people bashing.

13. **Attack issues not people.** When you need to correct team members, don't judge, demand, threaten, or moralize. Reject punishment as a successful behavior modification strategy. (51-53)

14. **Don't pit people against each other.** Someone once said that competition brings out the best in products and the worst in people. Team on team competitions can be a tonic. Person on person competitions can also be a tonic, but can quickly turn toxic. Why not instead reward people for cooperation with each other?

Breakthrough! Surely there is at least one action on this list that will minimize antagonism on your team. Which one is it, and how will you proceed?

When arguing with a stupid person, make sure he isn't doing the same thing.

~Author unknown

What is the best way to fight?

One-Minute Answer: A Chinese proverb says, "When you go to dig a grave for your enemy, dig two."

What an incredibly powerful statement this is about the need to fight right. If interpersonal conflict is played as a zero sum game where one side has to win while the other loses, the relationship *always* loses. Let's instead do our best to let the relationship win. We can put aside competition, prejudice, and old wounds to move to higher ground. (27-29)

Five-Minute Answer: When in disagreement with others, how well do the statements below describe your behavior? Use the following scale to rate your likelihood to act in each of these positive ways to resolve disagreement.

5 = Always **4** = Typically **3** = Often **2** = Sometimes **1** = Rarely **0** = Never

To get the most value from this self-assessment, complete it with regard to *two particular people* in your life. Person A might be at work and Person B might be at home. Score your behavior with each person on a sheet of paper. You stand to learn a great deal about the way you fight as you compare and contrast your approaches with these two different role players.

1. I enter into discussion with this person about our disagreement with the assumption that I bear significant responsibility—as much as 50%—for our conflict. (Guess what—you probably <u>do</u>!)

2. When I disagree, I am honest about the fact that I disagree, and why. I don't pretend that everything is okay when it isn't.

3. When proven wrong, I admit it rather than try to cover my tracks. I can easily say, "I was wrong." I am even capable of adding, "I am sorry."

4. I let the other person speak first to calm him or her down, reduce his or her need to talk, and learn what it will take to convince him or her. I have no problem listening to the other person's

assertions, and even accusations, getting my "two cents" in last. (It is foolish to go first and smart to go second in an argument.)

5. I stay calm and rational, focusing on issues, not personalities, and am careful not to say anything I'll regret later. (Talk is cheap, but you can't buy it back.)

6. When I allow myself to get angry, I talk about that anger rather than what the person did to elicit it. I recognize that this person has not *made* me angry—I have done it to myself.

7. Even as I disagree, I affirm the other person's right to his or her feelings. I neither think nor say anything like, "You have no business feeling that way."

8. My goal is to heal the relationship or solve a problem rather than prove the other person wrong. I strive for harmony in this relationship.

9. I direct our attention to fixing the future rather than rehashing the past. I don't harp on what this person did to hurt or disappoint me. I can state my pain once and then collaborate on a resolution.

10. I keep the focus on what each of us really needs in the situation, rather than what we merely want. This enables us to search for creative ways to meet both sets of needs even though our wants may appear at first to be totally incompatible and irreconcilable. ("Tell me what *you're* hoping to gain from this situation and I'll tell you what *I* would like to leave with.")

Analyzing the Results

Query 1: In what ways do you fight differently with each person? What do the greatest differences in scores tell you about the behavioral choices <u>you</u> are making that yield the comparative fruit you're harvesting with these two people?

Query 2: Do your overall scores suggest any ways to change how you fight? Which lowest scores scream the loudest for your attention?

Query 3: How else might you use this survey? Will you meet with the two people you chose in order to explain your self-ratings with a request for confirming or denying feedback from them? What if you asked others beyond these two to score you on the ten items?

Breakthrough! As you enter into your next disagreement with anyone in your work or personal life, in what one way will your behavior be different as a result of taking the assessment and analyzing the results?

Listening, not imitation, may be the sincerest form of flattery.

~Dr. Joyce Brothers

How can I become a better listener?

One-Minute Answer: Great listeners are great influencers.

The more that goes into your ears and is retained the more power and value you have in the relationships important to you. This is because...

A. **Your ear keeps your foot out of your mouth.** Leaders can't afford to sound stupid. Fully listen to and absorb questions, assertions, and emotions before you speak and you'll limit your diet of shoe leather.

B. **You learn what drives others.** In their conversations with you, people will reveal what makes them tick. As you listen non-judgementally they'll often share their vision, values, beliefs, opinions, desires, dreams, moods, aspirations, politics (watch out!), pain, and world view.

C. **You separate needs from wants.** Others often express a desire by saying, "I need..." When you respond with "How will it help to have that?" and then listen, their comeback is likely to state their true *need* as opposed to the *want* that they first blurted out. Why is this distinction important? If you satisfy a want, only rarely will the real underlying need also be met.

D. **You grow in knowledge.** You can't learn anything new when you're talking. The knowledge you gain with your ears is power.

E. **You defuse anger.** When you verbally engage angry people, there's a danger of escalating to their level of emotion and even beyond. Not good! When instead you lend an ear to those who are irate, you allow them to vent, to decompress to a calmer level of emotion, and to cooperate in mutual problem solving.

F. **You tell others they're important to you.** Consider how you'd feel if upon entering someone's office that person turns to an assistant and says, "Please hold my calls and protect us from interruptions." And what if when the door is closed that person looks you in the eye and says with sincerity, "How can I help you?"

And what if the conversation ends with you having consumed over 70% of the air time? Nice, huh?

G. **You encourage others to grow in intimacy with you.** Don't be thrown by the "i" word. In a professional relationship-building context intimacy means that the more people share matters of great importance to them with you the closer they'll feel toward you. The cooperation and service you'll receive will take off.

Five-Minute Answer: You'll reap the benefits expressed above once you become adept at *keeping people talking.* Here's how to do that.

1. **Wear an "open face."** Communication expert and coach Arch Lustberg demonstrates that lifting your eyebrows will elevate your tone of voice. (Try it!) Raised eyebrows yield an even greater communication benefit. They subconsciously signal to others that you're unconditionally open to their speech.

2. **Fashion a half smile.** The combination of an open face and a bit of a grin is dynamite encouragement for others to keep talking.

3. **Look into the eyes of the speaker.** This shows that you really do care about what's being said and adds, "Tell me more."

4. **Don't interrupt.** Restrain your opinions, objections, solutions, or any other judgement calls. When you constantly butt in the speaker concludes, "What's the use?" and clams up. Offer your ideas *after* the other person's point is made. You might even ask permission first.

5. **Stay focused.** You've been blessed with a listening capacity of about 480 words per minute; yet, most speaking occurs at only about 120 words per minute. Your excess listening power (360 wpm) is a barrier to understanding and retention when it tempts your mind to drift. As the resulting inattention causes your eyes to wander or glaze over, the speaker gets discouraged.

6. **Don't be doing anything else.** If you fiddle with something or are sitting at your computer quietly pushing the keys while participating in a telephone conversation, your tone of voice drops and reveals distance from the speaker.

7. **Share a task between you.** The best dialogues often occur between two people focused on a common undertaking. This advisory may at first appear to conflict with #6 above, but it doesn't. In this case, the activity that you're both engaged in stimulates the conversation.

8. **Paraphrase occasionally.** You'll tell the speaker you're listening and you'll tease out more information with, "Let me make sure I'm following; are you saying that...?"

9. **Empathize.** Often, people will bring their frustrations, failures, and fiascos to you. It can be very tempting to give advice, but only rarely will that advice be helpful. What is almost always helpful is to allow people to figure things out for themselves. A statement like, "That must be rough" or "You've got some challenges there" will encourage the other person to keep talking and thereby draw closer to *self* help—the best kind.

10. **Transform exclamation points into question marks.** When a speaker makes a strong statement such as, "...and I'm frustrated by that!" dead silence typically follows. Keep the conversation moving by repeating the last few words of the proclamation followed by a question mark. In the example above try, "Frustrated by that?" Invariably the speaker will regain momentum by saying something like "You bet! I..."

11. **Withhold "I," "me" or "my" from the first sentences of your responses.** Imagine someone tells you, "I've had a rough time today." Where would you go with that statement? Lousy listeners stop others in their tracks with, "I've had a difficult day myself." Great listeners keep the person talking with, "Tell me about it."

12. **Give someone a good listening-to.** Most of us have said, "I'm going to give her a good talking to." Few of us have ever said, "I'm going to give her a good listening-to." Review the One-Minute Answer above for the payoff.

Breakthrough! You may have already concluded that for the most part, listening is not a communication skill, it's primarily an *attitude*. If you want to do it badly enough and will *vow* to improve your oral comprehension of others, you'll make it happen. Great listening does not come naturally, nor does it need be learned—it is *willed*.

Asking the proper questions is the central action of transformation. Questions are the key that causes the secret doors of the psyche to swing open.

~Clarissa Pinkola Estes

How can I use questions for impact?

One-Minute Answer: The subtitle of my book, "What to Ask When You Don't Know What to Say" is "555 Powerful Questions to Use for Getting Your Way at Work." Since its release back in 1994, I have remained committed to the idea that questions are more commanding than statements.

First, they're different. When you ask a question of someone expecting a statement, you surprise them. In a heated conversation, for example, a person expecting a comeback to a spear of words just hurled at you will be thrown off balance by a reasoned question intended to resolve matters. The upper hand may be yours for the taking.

Second, you're not always in a position of sufficient authority to make a statement. By contrast, *anyone* can ask an authoritative question. In fact, a query is the best way to challenge what you see as a bad decision by a higher up. You might ask something like, "If when I suggest that resolution, the customer refuses to accept it, how do you want me handle that?"

Finally, questions are "magic." They turn confusion into clarity, resistance into receptivity, conflict into consensus, and silence into speech. When well stated, they can cause listeners to rethink their positions, to reflect on their behavior, and to open their minds to new possibilities.

Five-Minute Answer: Questions put you in charge of conversations in more than a few ways.

1. **They please hearers.** The right question shows consideration for and interest in the views of others. *How would you do that if you were me?*

2. **They focus thought.** Just as a lens condenses sunlight on a small spot, a question pinpoints thinking. *If you could flip a switch and change one thing about your current situation, what would that change be?*

3. **They harmonize conflicting views.** This is one of the essential steps to take in conflict resolution. *How do you see my needs being similar and dissimilar to yours?*

4. **They de-escalate anger and hostility.** When another person is agitated, your goal is to calm them. No statement will do this; only a question followed by non-judgemental listening. *How can I make it right?*

5. **They build friendships.** One of the best ways to nurture or even heal a relationship is to be a dedicated listener. *How did my action affect you?* (59-61)

6. **They inject accountability.** Accusations are rarely a good way to hold people responsible. Queries most often do a better job. *What measurable expectations should I have for the outcomes of your effort?*

7. **They display your commitment and interest.** Do this by asking "I care" questions. *What's the most important thing I need to know in order to serve you well?*

8. **They promote self-examination.** Any time you encourage others to look inside themselves for answers you perform a service to them. *If you were working in your ideal job right now, what would you be doing?*

9. **They convert wants into needs.** Most requests from bosses, customers, suppliers, colleagues, direct reports, children, spouses, siblings, parents, or friends are expressions of wants, even though they may be stated as "I need…" Turn those wants into needs and your responses will be more satisfying to the requestor. *What is it that you'll achieve by having it done that way?*

10. **They remove the sting from criticism.** There is certainly nothing wrong with a statement of well-delivered, constructive criticism. ("I discovered this morning that the front door was left unlocked all night.") But asking a question often assures that the recipient will not feel attacked, and it may even help you discover an acceptable explanation for your grievance. *Is there a reason why the front door would have been left unlocked all night?* (51-53)

Breakthrough! There is a certain three-fold art to asking good questions.

First, if you have been a good listener all along, your questions will fit into the context of the situation and will therefore make good sense to the hearer. (Speaking of listening, be sure to do that when your question is answered!)

Second, a supportive and genuinely inquisitive tone in your asking voice will prevent defensiveness.

Third, certain questions need to have their sharp edges smoothed before the asking. Soften otherwise confrontive questions with: "May I ask...?" or "There's something I've been wondering about."

The medium is the message.

~Marshall McLuhan

What do I need to know about body language?

One-Minute Answer: In a widely referenced communication study, UCLA Professor Albert Mehrabian discovered that words contain only 7% of the power that can be unleashed through face-to-face communication. Another 38% of our influence is attributed to voice, with body language accounting for a clear majority—55% of our conversational impact.

When I read his study back in the 70's my immediate reaction was, "There's no way that words account for only 7% of the impression we make on our listeners!" After four more decades of life experience I still say, "No way." There's no way words register *that much* force!

Consider this exercise that undergraduate students experienced in an Organizational Communication course at the University of Pittsburgh. Five of my male colleagues, invited into a class, sat in the front of the room saying nothing. They were intentionally differentiated in apparel, accessories, posture, facial characteristics, and body movement. Students were given a survey on which to rate how well each of the five men fit these descriptions: (1) easy to get to know; (2) intelligent; (3) assertive; (4) wealthy; (5) flexible; (6) moody; (7) reliable. Over the years 500+ students effortlessly completed the survey without anyone ever pushing back. Not one student said, "You can't expect me to make these judgements based only on appearances." People just as easily do the same thing to you.

Five-Minute Answer: Become more mindful of your body language through the answers to these questions.

1. **Why do I get in trouble for the emails I send?** The most likely reason is that you're exercising only 7% of your potential impact. Recipients of your message can't read your face, your stance, and your gestures to understand what you really mean by the words they see on their screen.

2. **What's the only part of my body I can't lie with?** An Arabic proverb says, "The eyes are the portals to the soul." Your eyes reveal whether you're happy or heavyhearted, credible or crooked, swayed or skeptical, attentive or abstracted.

3. **Why does a fake smile look that way?** Failing to experience the emotion that would set off a smile keeps your *eyes* from smiling. The mouth is far less a contributor to facial joy.

4. **Why do State Troopers wear reflective sun glasses?** Putting a visual shield between the two of you confines the writing of your speeding ticket to official business. We bond with others through eye contact—something an officer of the law wants to avoid, but something you covet in so many of your relationships.

5. **Can I use my body to listen better?** Turn toward people when they talk to you and look them in the eyes. Lift your eyebrows slightly to open your face. If the other person is sitting, sit. If the other person is standing, stand.

6. **Can I use my body to sell better?** When I make sales calls, I'm careful that my body language is not noticeably incongruent with prospects. If they're leaning forward I won't lean back. If their legs aren't crossed I won't cross mine. If they're sitting still I'm determined not to fidget. I do the research to ensure my dress will be consistent with theirs. I even adjust my handshake in mid grasp to their firmness.

7. **Can I use my body to keep people talking?** When others put you on the spot with their requests, their questions, or with their personal problems keep them talking. Find out what they really need before you offer your thoughts or a solution. Elevate your eyebrows a half-inch slightly and sprout a half smile. You'll be amazed at how much this encourages sharing.

8. **How can I become more persuasive in a meeting?** According to research the power of your ideas will rise about 75% if you stand up, walk to a flipchart or whiteboard, and write or draw your ideas as you speak. The combined impact of standing up and of visualizing your thoughts advances your position.

9. **How do mirrors mislead me?** Many years ago my little girl looked on as I straightened my tie in front of my wife's dresser. As I primped she said, "Don't bother Daddy. Our teacher told us that what you see in a mirror isn't what other people see. It's backwards." She was right! Since none of us have perfectly symmetrical hair, faces, etc., what *we* see isn't what *they* get.

10. **What's the most dangerous gesture?** Pointing at people. This is a demeaning, controlling, and attacking act of aggression. Instead, put all four digits together. Gesture toward the person you're singling out with an open palm.

11. **What handshake isolates me from others?** Your palm is a highly sensitive part of your body. When it touches the palm of another, a close physical bond results. When, instead, you offer a cupped hand you distance yourself from those you greet.

12. **What does my office say?** When people enter your office (your car or your home) they're bombarded by messages beyond those radiating from you. While your desktop is certainly a message sender, two other variables compete for attention. One is how you arrange your furniture, thereby controlling where they stand or sit as they converse with you. Another is what you hang on your walls, thereby revealing your inner-most values.

13. **What does my clothing say?** Imagine what people really hear if they're thinking any of these thoughts. "Who's he trying to impress?" "She must not think much of herself dressed that way." "Doesn't he realize we do business casual?" "I wonder if she owns a can of shoe polish?" "Is he color blind?"

14. **Is body odor an element of body language?** Is heat an element of the sun? Men need to find a deodorant that really works. Women need to be sure that their cologne or perfume is not overbearing. Everyone needs to know if they should take action to control bad breath. Ask someone who you trust to be honest with you about how you might be offending.

15. **Why do people fold their arms over their chest?** I have no idea. The classic interpretation is being closed to your ideas or feeling protective. Maybe so, but an arm-folder may also be cold, tired, or experiencing an angina attack. We cannot read body language with perfect accuracy in the absence of other confirming cues. Besides, the insights above were not provided to teach you how to read others. Instead, they alert you to the shouts of your body that compete mightily with your words.

Breakthrough! Learn more about your 55%. Pick one item from the list above each week to monitor in your communication with others.

Do not use a hatchet to remove a fly from your friend's forehead.

~Japanese proverb

How can I do a better job of delivering criticism?

One-Minute Answer: When you open your mouth to remedy performance, your words will hold either more power than sting or more sting than power. Your words contain power when the recipient is encouraged to engage in the new behavior you ask for. They possess sting when the receiver feels attacked, invalidated, or singled out.

The prescriptions below will help you maximize the power and minimize the sting. Notice that I say *minimize* the sting, not *eliminate* it. You know yourself that the kindest rebuke you ever received hurt, even if just a little. So, expect an initially self-protective response to even the most constructively offered criticism. You may have to wait a while for the sting to subside and the power to kick in. If the power never kicks in one of two situations exists: either you've encountered a highly sensitive person who'll be stung by most any attempt at correction or you need to revisit the advice below, apologize for your error, and try again.

Five-Minute Answer: Here are six practices that will turn you into a deliverer of constructive, power-producing criticism. When you apply them to your life you'll put into practice the celebrated one liner: "Condemn the deed, not the doer."

1. **Do it in private!** Whenever I ask a group of employees if they recall ever being criticized by their boss in public, a third to a half of the hands go up. When I ask how many believe they will ever forget that event, very few hands fall. Even though some say they forgive the boss for that indiscretion, it has been burned into their psyche. If there is an "unpardonable leadership sin" this is it.

2. **Avoid the pronoun "you."** Every time "you" is the first word out of your mouth, you're the king (or queen) of sting. A far better beginning pronoun is "I." Consider three possible approaches for an employee who just submitted to you a sloppily prepared report. Try this *I see* opener: "I discovered seven typos in the quarterly report." Try this *I feel* opener: "I was disappointed to find seven typos in the quarterly report." Or, try this *I need*

opener. "I can't present to my boss a quarterly report containing seven typos."

3. **Examine your heart before you open your mouth.** You can't mask what's in your heart with cleverly chosen words. If you're angry or in *any* negative emotional state, your tone and your body language will give you away and lead to sting. If that outcome is acceptable, go right ahead. But if you want a different (power) result, picture what you want that result to be. See it in that person's face and hear it in that person's response. Ask yourself, "Is how I'm feeling about this situation going to elicit that desired impact?" If not, get your heart right first. Take a walk, allow some time, or pray for calmness before you speak your mind. (47-49)

4. **Ask a question.** There are three reasons why the first words out of your mouth might be a question, not a statement. **First,** you may not have all the facts in the situation that the answer to a question might reveal. **Second,** a lead off question is one way to start off in the direction of power rather than sting. In the quarterly report example consider, "Is there something that would help me understand why there are seven typos in this quarterly report?" **Third,** if you lack authority in a situation— e.g., with a boss—the answer to your question often enables you to go where you were reluctant to start. For a boss who micromanages try, "What can I do to earn your trust?" and work with the answer you get. (43-45)

5. **Attack behavior, not attitude.** As a leader, you'll never encounter an attitude problem. Yes, you read that right! You'll only encounter *behavior* problems. An attitude becomes a problem only when that attitude manifests itself in the form of negative behavior. In fact, employee attitudes about anything— punctuality, performance, people, you name it—are really none of your business. What *is* your business is their performance. So never think or say, "You need to change your attitude about _____." Instead, insist on the behavior necessary for teamwork, for adherence to policy, for safety, for efficiency, for goal achievement, for fulfillment of stated expectations—for *any* required actions.

6. **Apply the "John Wooden Rule".** John Wooden was arguably the most successful college basketball coach ever. From 1964 to 1975

he led his UCLA Bruins to an incredible ten NCAA Championships. Of the many ingredients to his coaching effectiveness, one was uncovered by educational physiologists given access to Bruin practices in order to study his leadership style. The researchers were taken aback by how Wooden criticized his players when he caught them in the act of making a mistake. If, for example, he witnessed a player dribbling improperly, he'd shout the player's name. Then he would say something like, "Let me show you how we dribble at UCLA" or "Let me show you how you can dribble through five players and they'll never touch the ball." John Wooden was turning criticism opportunities into teaching moments. Sound like you?

Breakthrough! I'm a big fan of having at my fingertips ("liptips?") a handful of scripts that are consistent with the principles above as well as other best criticism practices. In the heat of battle, I don't always have the presence of mind to apply the principles well; it's easier for me to rely on proven scripts for the half dozen or so performance disappointments I most often encounter. Pick a few from this list for your own use and add ones appropriate for the situations you typically face.

"Kim, I just observed an interaction with one of our customers that could have gone much better."

"Jerry, I need to count on you to…"

"Joan, let me show you how to make that work."

"Peter, it's not like you to…"

"Sara, I feel let down by these results"

"Gino, help me understand why…"

"Jan, what'll it take to keep this from happening again?"

Good bosses make their people think they have more ability than they have, so they consistently do better work than they thought they could.

~Charles E. Wilson

How can I use praise more effectively to motivate others?

One-Minute Answer: The Chief Operations Officer of a company serving over 250,000 corporate clients was diligent about convening a brief monthly gathering of his entire local staff. These were wonderful meetings held in response to suggestions received on an earlier employee survey. At one of the meetings I happened to attend, Jack (not his real name) did his usual fine job of feeding people yummy treats, making useful announcements, acknowledging employee milestones, and giving attendees every opportunity to ask questions—answered masterfully.

At one point Jack graciously acknowledged the fine work of Amber (not her real name) who had just organized the most successful international training conference in firm history. He fairly gushed over her results and the positive impact they had on corporate goals. He led the group in applause for her efforts.

Given the leadership advice he had received from me and others, Jack was pleased with his handling of the meeting, and wasn't prepared for what happened next. Before 5 PM that day, two people from the meeting had come in to see him and five others had marched into the office of the Director of HR, all with like grievances. Can you guess what they were?

Five-Minute Answer: Do you desire to take full advantage of the motivational power of your praise? If so, use the ideas that follow. You'll know when you've arrived at Jack's mistake(s) even before I tell you.

1. **Be sincere.** Don't praise merely because I or anyone else tells you that it's a good idea. Acknowledgment must stem from an earnest desire to lift a person up. If that doesn't feel right to you, the conniving nature of your commendation will be easily discovered and resolutely resented.

2. **Don't pass it out like candy.** Scarcity equals value. If you praise too much, it can lose its value. But don't worry about this one. I have yet to hear of such a case in all my years of leadership coaching. I did see a movie once where it was a problem.

3. **Keep it short.** You may remember that the best-selling book *The One Minute Manager* referred to one-minute praisings. Don't do it! Praise someone for that long and they'll upchuck on your shoes. It takes one-half second to say, "Thank you." If you want to splurge, it takes two seconds to say, "You did a great job on that report." If you have as many as four seconds to spare, go for "I appreciate your willingness to stay late in order for us to meet that deadline."

4. **Drop your skepticism.** Don't wait to see more of a behavior before paying tribute to it: "I'll say something when I'm sure it's permanent." Don't feel entitled to the behavior: "It's about time!" Don't be suspicious of a sudden improvement: "What's she up to now?"

5. **Don't negate it.** Never follow congratulations with "Make sure you keep it that way," "It's about time", or even "Keep up the good work." The best thing you can do after honoring improvement is to disappear. Don't give one and take two back. Don't blow up the balloon and then stick a pin in it.

6. **Praise the deed, not the doer.** You've learned "Condemn the deed, not the doer" as a constructive criticism principle. (51-53) Guess what! The same is true for praise. What do you want your people to be turned on by? You? No! Themselves? No! Their work? *Yes!* So extol their work, not them.

7. **Write a note of thanks.** A permanent record of your approval means much. One that comes from your hand will mean even more than one that rolls off a laser printer or pops up in an email. I have seen such notes framed and hanging in cubicles.

8. **Post an entry in the employee's personnel file.** Some employees find warnings and disciplinary letters in their dossiers; almost no one discovers appreciation there.

9. **Thank people for not doing the wrong thing.** You read this right! Your leadership role occasionally calls upon you to convert behavior from dysfunctional to functional, from unproductive to productive, and from troublesome to trouble free. When as a result of your coaching, employees succeed at any of these transformations, they'll be looking for appreciation of the favor they feel they have done for you. Zero thanks from you will be

interpreted as not caring about them or their improvement. Expect back-sliding to result.

10. **Get people's names out there.** You've heard that *what* you know doesn't matter as much as *who* you know. But even more important than who you know is *who knows you*. One the most valued forms of acknowledgment is to showcase your people in the company, in the community, and even in the industry. Do you allow the accomplishments (the light) of your rising stars to be widely seen? Or do you allow fear of losing them tempt you to hide them under a bushel basket?

11. **"Gossip" about them.** For every two times you praise someone, say something nice to others about that person. There's only one thing that great leaders do behind people's backs—pat them.

12. **Replace "employee of the month" with "team of the month".** It always amazes me that while we pay great lip service to teamwork, we subvert that goal by extolling the virtues of individual effort over that of a team. You'll see next why this was part of Jack's lapse of judgement.

13. **Be careful where you do it.** Somewhere along the way Jack apparently heard and bought into the adage, "Condemn in private, praise in public." He learned the hard way how poorly this idea can fare in practice. Indeed, Amber had done a great job on the training conference, but she didn't do it alone. Hearers of public praise who are not receivers are prone to one of three reactions: "What about the contribution *I* made?" "He never praises *me* that way." "*Teacher's pet!*"

Breakthrough! Find three people in your life who need a word of encouragement from you. Plan the encounter in a way that honors the guidance above.

Life is relationships; the rest is just deals.

~Gary Smalley

What is the best advice for improving relationships?

One-Minute Answer: We were made to be in relationship—at home, at work, and everywhere in our existence. The connections we make with others elevate our productivity as well as our service to others. When those connections are close and satisfying, the teams we join are more successful and our individual lives are more joyful.

The benefits of healthy relationships have been known since the beginning of humanity.

> Consider the following. We humans are social beings. We come into the world as the result of others' actions. We survive here in dependence on others. Whether we like it or not, there is hardly a moment of our lives when we do not benefit from others' activities. For this reason it is hardly surprising that most of our happiness arises in the context of our relationships with others.
> *~Tenzin Gyatso, 14th Dalai Lama*

> In poverty and other misfortunes of life, true friends are a sure refuge. The young they keep out of mischief; to the old they are a comfort and aid in their weakness, and those in the prime of life they incite to noble deeds.   *~Aristotle*

> Shared joy is a double joy; shared sorrow is half a sorrow.
> *~Swedish Proverb*

Five-Minute Answer: You have a personal association somewhere in your life to enjoy more fully. Read on for what it might take to do that.

Ways We Suffer When not in Relationship

"The experience of separateness arouses anxiety; it is, indeed, the source of all anxiety."   ~Erich Fromm

"Solitude: A good place to visit, but a poor place to stay."
~Josh Billings

"Hatred paralyzes life; love releases it. Hatred confuses life; love harmonizes it. Hatred darkens life; love illuminates it."

~*Martin Luther King Jr.*

"I think everybody should get rich and famous and do everything they ever dreamed of so they can see that it's not the answer."

~*Jim Carrey*

Mistakes to Avoid

"Sticks and stones are hard on bones
Aimed with angry art,
Words can sting like anything
But silence breaks the heart."

~*Phyllis McGinley*

"Assumptions are the termites of relationships."

~*Henry Winkler*

"Present your family and friends with their eulogies now; they won't be able to hear how much you love them and appreciate them from inside the coffin."

~*Anonymous*

"Trouble is part of your life, and if you don't share it, you don't give the person who loves you enough chance to love you enough."

~*Dinah Shore*

"People change and forget to tell each other."

~*Lillian Hellman*

"When a friend is in trouble. Don't annoy him by asking if there is anything you can do. Think up something appropriate and do it."

~*Edward W. Howe*

"In the end, who among us does not choose to be a little less right to be a little less lonely."

~*Robert Brault*

"If it's very painful for you to criticize your friends, you're safe in doing it. But if you take the slightest pleasure in it, that's the time to hold your tongue."

~*Alice Duer Miller*

Attitudes and Actions that Build Bonds

"I know in my heart that man is good. That what is right will always eventually triumph. And there's purpose and worth to each and every life."

~*Ronald Regan*

"Life has taught us that love does not consist of gazing at each other, but in looking together in the same direction."

~*Antoine de Saint-Exupéry*

"Oh, the comfort— the inexpressible comfort— of feeling safe with a person, having neither to weigh thoughts nor measure words, but pouring them all right out, just as they are, chaff and grain together; certain that a faithful hand will take and sift them, keep what is worth keeping, and then with the breath of kindness blow the rest away."   ~*Arabic proverb*

"We make a living by what we get; we make a life by what we give."
                                                                    ~*Winston Churchill*

"How far you go in life depends on your being tender with the young, compassionate with the aged, sympathetic with the striving and tolerant of the weak and strong. Because someday in life you will have been all of these."   ~*George Washington Carver*

"If you were going to die soon and had only one phone call you could make, who would you call and what would you say? And why are you waiting?"   ~*Stephen Levine*

...and Don't Forget Empathy and Forgiveness

"In the course of my life, I have often had to eat my words, and I must confess that I have always found it a wholesome diet."
                                                                    ~*Winston Churchill*

"I will not criticize another until I have walked a mile in his moccasins."   ~*American Indian proverb*

"Forgiveness is the economy of the heart...forgiveness saves the expense of anger, the cost of hatred, the waste of spirits."
                                                                    ~*Hannah More*

"Write the bad things that happen to you in sand, but write the good things that happen to you on a piece of marble."   ~*Arabic proverb*

"Do not judge, and you will not be judged. Do not condemn, and you will not be condemned. Forgive and you will be forgiven."
                                                                    ~*Luke 6:37*

Breakthrough! Which of your relationships do you vow to heal? What new, renewed, or extinguished behavior inspired by the ideas above will you apply?

Rare is the man who can weigh the faults of others without putting his thumb on the scales.

~Laurence J. Peter

When do performance appraisals fail to improve performance?

One-Minute Answer: Companies commit to formal performance appraisals with one, or both, of two ends in mind. The first is to document performance so they can justify actions like pay raises, promotions, and terminations. Many systems, with a heavy emphasis on quantification of performance, do an efficient job of this.

A second and far nobler purpose is *to improve performance.* I've surveyed hundreds of managers regarding their beliefs that the performance reviews conducted within their companies improve performance. From their snickers, lowered heads, or sheepish "no's," I've concluded that few systems, if any, spur employees on to better execution of their duties.

When I ask these same managers to describe the emotions they experience during the evaluation experience, the most common report is of knots in the stomach. It's no wonder so many of them push back on the deadlines HR sets for them to complete annual reviews of employees.

Five-Minute Answer: Here are the issues at the root of failure of most corporate performance review systems. How does yours fare?

1. **They are yearly in "spirit."** The typical frequency of formal performance reviews is yearly. Semi-annually or even quarterly is better, but often impractical. Yearly is okay, but too many managers conclude that they are to speak to employees only once a year about their performance. To the contrary, downward feedback should be so abundant that the formal review does little more than confirm both the criticism and praise that has been showered on the employee throughout the year. (51-57)

2. **Assessments fail to mirror the company's core values.** One dimension on which to evaluate employees is the measurable outcomes of their efforts toward specific team and company goal achievement (the "what"). It assesses whether they're getting the right amount and quality of product out the door. The second dimension begging for appraisal is the degree to which employee behavior adheres to the core values of the organization (the

"how"). It judges whether they're getting product out the door without leaving bodies behind in their wake. If your company has articulated core values, create a section on the performance review to measure adherence to those values. (83-85)

3. **Managers are not trained to use the methodology consistently.** No manager should hold employees to a higher or lower standard than other managers. This training would also address the need to provide ongoing feedback (#1 above) as well as how to do it. (51-57)

4. **Managers won't submit reviews on time.** HR professionals will tell you that one of their greatest sources of frustration is reviewers who refuse to give this process a high priority, perform it thoughtfully, or meet its deadlines. Where the corporate culture doesn't encourage managers to comply, top management may have to impose negative consequences on slackers.

5. **Managers don't appraise courageously.** At the break of a presentation I made to 200 executives in Pittsburgh, an audience member approached me for a private conversation. At the age of 60 he had just been assigned to a new boss who had given him by far the worst evaluation of his extended tenure with the same company. He was crushed and bonus-less. Another evaluation like this one could jeopardize his ability to retire from that organization. By the end of the conversation, my sixth sense told me that this poor man had for the first time in a career of mediocre accomplishment been evaluated honestly. How unfair those earlier bosses had been to someone for whom it was now too late to transform.

6. **Employees have no opportunity to perform a self-evaluation.** Employees who have thought through the dimensions of evaluation prior to a performance review conference will take away more. But, the self-evaluation strategy needs to be such that there is no argumentative confrontation or a quibbling over numbers. Comparisons of self-evaluations to manager evaluations should not be structured to encourage debates of whether an employee earned a "3" or a "4" on a particular scale.

7. **Numerical scores are a prominent feature.** Here's an encounter that should never happen—but does all the time! An employee leaving a performance review meeting in your office

runs into a colleague, who asks, "Whadja get?" The answer, "Not too bad. I averaged 4.2." To which the colleague responds, "4.2! She gave me a 3.7—that's not fair!" If your performance review system emphasizes numbers and their importance, that's what employees will care about. Another likely utterance from the recipient of the 4.2 is, "I'm safe for another year."

8. **Phrases that replace numbers often don't help.** One of my clients proudly sports an "enlightened" performance rating system that eschews numbers. Employees are either U: Unacceptable; NI: Needs improvement; ME: Meets expectations; EE: Exceeds expectations; or SEE: Significantly exceeds expectations. Two things are wrong here. First, I once heard a senior manager disparagingly refer to a candidate for promotion as being merely an "ME"—a label that employee carried until the next review. It's demeaning to label people! The second problem is explained by your answer to this question: How do you feel about employees who fully meet every one of your expectations? *Ecstatic!* You're going to disappoint that employee with an "ME"?

9. **The form functions principally as a report card of the past.** Instead of "here's how you did," the discussion should focus on "here's what you need to do." Rather than focus on quantitative scores received, effective evaluations point employees to *the behaviors required to move them to the next highest level*. Even if your system is designed to be a report card, you can fix that by focusing employees on what they need to start, stop, and continue doing in order to achieve a higher evaluation next time.

10. **The dreaded "bell curve" holds sway.** Forcing ratings into a normal distribution or other statistical standard, ties the hands of managers who have developed—or are blessed with—particularly outstanding employees. This is often a source of discouragement.

11. **Higher ups override evaluations given by direct reports.** This is a sure way to cut the legs out from under junior managers. Any lack of trust in their decision making ought to be resolved outside the context of their judgement on performance reviews.

Breakthrough! What ideas do you now have for revising or leveraging your appraisal process to impact performance more favorably?

The closest to perfection a person ever comes is when he fills out a job application.

~Stanley Randall

How can I avoid hiring mistakes?

One-Minute Answer: Hiring the wrong person is a costly blunder. The opportunity lost when another choice would have performed better depresses the bottom line. The pain of squandered resources, team disruption, and legal issues are excruciating. Unnecessary time spent dealing with problem hires and finding replacements is permanent.

Two-thirds of all new hires are regretted. Why? Because we rely on unreliable criteria to make selections among the resumes our recruiters generate. And what are two of the worst predictors of job success? *Education and Experience*

There is no way to know what a person has taken away from that impressive looking degree. Who's to say that the A's on a transcript will translate into performance on a job? And there are two kinds of applicants—those who have ten years of experience and those who have *one year of experience repeated ten times.*

So, if we pay less attention to conventional credentials, what criteria should take their place?

Five-Minute Answer: Someone quipped that employees are most transparent during their exit interview and most deceptive during their employment interview. Here's how to examine a "best foot forward" more carefully:

1. **Hope for the best answer to the question...** As General Manager Barbara McMahon planned the opening of the Pittsburgh Renaissance Hotel in 2001 she knew her most crucial hires would be in housekeeping. So she personally interviewed candidates along with the head of that department. Barbara prized one question above all others in uncovering winners. It was, "What do you like best about housekeeping?" The answer she wanted to hear was, "What the room looks like when I leave it." What answer do you hope to hear to, "What do you like best about...?

2. **Give a job sample test.** If you're hiring trainers, watch them train. If you're hiring managers, give them paperwork you've been dealing with for their advice. If you're hiring architects, let

them critique the plans for a current project. Barbara McMahon caused housekeeping aspirants to pass a crumpled piece of paper on the floor as they walked into her office for the interview.

3. **Check references wisely.** Get reliable data from references by creating a list of your ten most coveted qualities for the position. Read them over the phone in rapid fire as the reference rates the candidate from one to ten on each quality. For the two or three higher scores go back to ask what the person did to earn them; for the two or three lower scores, dig deep. Another reason to call references is to verify information. Consider telling the candidate whom you plan to call and ask what she thinks each person will say about her performance. This increases honesty.

4. **Leverage your stars.** Ask your top performers to refer friends for open positions. Get feedback from them after they give all interviewees an office tour or take them to lunch.

5. **Perform pre-employment testing.** A wide battery of tests is available on-line to improve your decisions. They measure: (1) aptitude in math, language, typing, and reasoning; (2) cognitive ability to analyze and solve problems; (3) personality characteristics and emotional intelligence; (4) attitude toward honesty, theft, and drugs; (5) psychomotor skills, coordination, and manual dexterity; (6) physical capabilities such as lifting. Before leveraging the benefits of pre-employment testing, get the help of an expert to manage its complexity and avoid any legal traps.

6. **Seek culture fit.** A huge reason for the failure of new hires is their mismatch with the norms of behavior in your organization. If you have a set of core values, a team charter, or published performance expectations, do this: Tell the candidate that no one in the company performs equally well on all of the core values, team charter items, or performance expectations. Direct him to choose two or three items from the list that he expects will be easier than the rest to fulfill with distinction and explain his choices. Next, ask for two or three that will be more challenging than the rest. These choices and their explanations are accurate indicators of culture fit. (15-17; 83-85)

7. **Look for teach-ability.** One reason new employees don't mesh

with company culture is that they're set in their ways, they believe they have little to learn, or they "know" they're in the right. Ask this: "Name three things you need to get better at and tell me what your plan is for achieving each one."

8. **Look for fire in the belly.** Does this person's application and her presence reveal a high sense of urgency, a compelling desire to succeed, and a dedication to continuous improvement.

9. **Look for integrity.** This is a difficult quality to assess in advance of employment. Include "integrity" or "honesty" as one of the ten qualities you read off during the reference check described above. One of my favorite interview questions is, "Why is it important to do the right thing?" (e.g., Why is it important to perform honest audits, or be completely truthful with clients?) The reassuring answer is, "Because it's the right thing to do."

10. **Look for resistance to bashing.** Is it easy to get the candidate to condemn others? Get a response to this: "We all find challenges from time to time working for a difficult boss or collaborating with problem peers. Describe the worst such relationship you've encountered at work." If a candidate easily trashes others, end the interview.

11. **Find a team player.** Is this candidate more eager to demonstrate his talents or to work together with others to make the company a success? Does his background show an interest in team play? Is there evidence of strong interpersonal skills? What is revealed when you ask, "When I assess your job performance, how much should I rely on your excellence as a mechanical engineer versus your ability to work well with the other engineers?"

12. **Hire a vet!** Put a man or woman who has returned from service to country at the head of the line. Military life instills leadership, tests ability to deal with adversity, values integrity, turns out team players, places a high value on work ethic, teaches conflict resolution, breeds toughness, squelches a sense of entitlement, and accustoms men and women to taking orders—not mindlessly, yet without knee-jerk counter-dependence.

Breakthrough! Incorporate these ideas into a workshop for those in your company who make selection decisions. Use them yourself.

So in everything, do to others what you would have them do to you, for this sums up the Law and the Prophets.

~Matthew 7:12

What role do manners and civility play in the workplace?

One-Minute Answer: At the tender age of 14, George Washington crafted 110 rules for life. He titled them *Rules of Civility & Decent Behaviour in Company and Conversation.* His advice remains as pertinent as it was in 1746 America. Here are three of my favorites:

1. Every action done in company ought to be with some sign of respect to those that are present.

35. Let your discourse with men of business be short and comprehensive.

110. Labour to keep alive in your breast that little celestial fire called conscience.

The question above was prompted by Washington's rules. It also responds to complaints from people who respect tradition and long for earlier values of manners and civility in the office and certainly the home. From listening to those wishes, and sharing them myself, I've drafted my own inventory of desirable conduct in the workplace.

Prepare yourself for 22 prescriptions in three groupings: respect, communications, and relationships. And yes, one of them does speak to colleagues who text or twitter in the meetings you attend.

Five-Minute Answer: Imagine that you work closely with someone who follows little of the advice below. (I hope you have to strain very hard to do this!) How does that affect your job satisfaction? Well, guess what? Many others are as affected by the same rudeness, thoughtlessness, and inconsideration—hopefully not from you.

Read through the list below. Put a check mark (√) in the boxes in front of those descriptions you are absolutely sure consistently characterize your behavior. Use a question mark (?) where you're not sure or the item only sometimes describes you. Put an (X) in front of the behaviors that you violate more often than you and others want to see. Leave blank those items not applicable or unclear to you.

Respect toward Others

- [ ] I work collaboratively and deferentially with senior management. (99-101)
- [ ] I submit to those in authority. 103-105)
- [ ] I arrive to meetings on time and stay the whole time, unless excused.
- [ ] In meetings, I keep my PDA and laptop computer turned off except to receive critical phone calls or to participate in the meeting.
- [ ] I attend retreats and conferences scheduled for my team; I don't look for excuses to leave early.
- [ ] I attend and participate actively in training sessions paid for by my employer.
- [ ] In every way, I respect the time, schedules, and workloads of others.

Communicating with Others

- [ ] My speech is seasoned with grace; not peppered with demeaning, sarcastic, profane, or degrading language.
- [ ] I say my piece once and move on; I'm succinct and crisp; I don't bloviate.
- [ ] I'm careful to adjust the expression of my thoughts to the sensibilities, needs, and demographics of the particular person listening to me.
- [ ] I listen when others speak, rather than interrupt, finish their sentences, or merely wait to seize air time. (39-41)
- [ ] I don't eavesdrop or barge into other's conversations; I respect their privacy.
- [ ] I won't speak in a language, or use terminology, others don't understand in front of them.
- [ ] I'm not a gossip; neither do I violate confidences.
- [ ] My speech brims with "please", "hello", "excuse me", "thank you" and "my pleasure".

Relationship Building (49-60)

☐ I smile, give eye contact, and greet others when I encounter them. (47-49)

☐ I provide a timely answer or response to people when they put the ball in my court.

☐ I fulfill my promises and obligations or alert others quickly that I can't.

☐ I express any concerns I may have about people's behavior to them and not to others.

☐ I am tactful yet directly honest about my positions, opinions, feelings, and beliefs.

☐ I ask, "Will you forgive me?" when I have disappointed, hurt, or offended others.

☐ I am not demanding nor do I exert unwanted influence or dominance over others.

Breakthrough! What did you learn in your self-assessment? Is there a role player in your life who you now realize will welcome changed behavior from you? Consider other ways to use this list. Is there someone, or even a team, you can ask for confirmation on your checks, questions marks, and X's? Might a few of these statements find a place on your team charter? (15-17) Might this list form the foundation of a mandatory training class for the employees of your company? Are you now emboldened to give feedback to someone whose lack of decorum troubles you? (51-53)

If a house be divided against itself, that house cannot stand.

~Mark 3:25

How do we get people out of their silos?

One-Minute Answer: Some fear that environmental changes now sweeping the planet, such as the loss of forests and the spread of cities, are promoting conditions for a rise in new and previously suppressed infectious diseases.

In the same way, there's reason to believe that a steady erosion of decisive leadership, economic conditions that focus managers on survival, and business's growing love affair with matrix organizational structures is spawning an insidious corporate sickness. The diagnosis is *suboptimization.*

Suboptimization is present when division managers and team leaders strive to optimize the results of their own units without much concern for the negative outcomes that their actions may produce for other units. The end result is that while they indeed optimize outcomes—their own—they repeatedly trigger reduced (suboptimal) outcomes for the total organization. For example, the procurement team may insist that the sales team jump through hoops to maintain order in the procurement system, but as a result prevent sales people from getting back quickly to their customers. This is more commonly known as "silo" behavior.

Suboptimization is rampant in organizations where managers are evaluated strictly on the performance of their own departments and when they're given reason to fear the repercussions of failing to outperform other departments. Managers who are highly competitive and who hold themselves to the highest standards of performance are particularly vulnerable.

Five-Minute Answer: Take the medicine from this list that you believe will cure the suboptimization infecting your teams.

1. Author Robert Byrne once said, "The purpose of life is a life of purpose." Give your departments/teams a powerful common purpose (a desirable future, a fantastic dream, an inspiring vision, a glorious cause)—one that will unite them and demonstrate their mutual interests. Though two teams may have distinctively different missions (e.g., Finance and HR) they can

be united through a common cause (e.g., create the most cost effective workforce).

2. Hire people with a positive attitude, an energetic approach, and a can-do spirit. Employees with such an emotional bent are far more likely to collaborate with others across the company than those who see the glass as half empty with a hole in the bottom.

3. Establish teamwork as a corporate core value. Go beyond merely paying lip service to the idea by making it one of the key measures on your performance review document. Provide both positive and negative consequences for adherence to it—particularly the inter-team variety.

4. Insist as much upon incomparable internal customer service as you require extraordinary external customer service. Preach it regularly and loudly. Define internal customer service so people know what it is. Conduct workshops on the topic so people know how to provide it.

5. Address any lack of cooperation or conflict among team leaders. Their relationships are key to the collaboration among their direct reports. Here's a conflict resolution tool used recently with department heads Ralph and Katie (names changed), which has had positive repercussions throughout their divisions. First, they were asked in sequence to write on a flip chart in full view the main five to ten expectations they believed the other had of them. Second, they each confirmed the degree to which the other correctly guessed their expectations. Each one then edited his or her list to have a perfect statement of the actual expectations held of the other. Third, I asked them to rate how fully each expectation that they have of the other is being met. Fourth, Ralph and Katie then each made vows for new, renewed, or extinguished behavior for the three expectations that the other believed were being least fulfilled. We've had several follow up meetings since to assess their progress and hold them accountable for progress.

6. Keep all of your teams well aware of change in the industry, in customer demands, and in the rest of the company. This way they'll be less surprised by, and therefore less resistant to, non-routine requests from other departments that stem from such change.

7. Rotate employees throughout your organization. The best servant to an outside team is someone who once worked on it.

8. When rotation is not practical, see that the members of every team are educated on the mission, processes, and expectations of every other group with which they need to collaborate.

9. Engage your senior leadership team in a strategic planning exercise that forces them to reach consensus on strategic priorities as well as on the collaborative actions from their departments required to achieve the priorities and actions.

10. See that your senior leadership team drafts a Team Charter that asserts the valid requirements they should have of each other. Ensure that it remains a living, breathing document. (15-17)

11. Benchmark other companies like yours that have had great success in building internal customer service. Study them carefully to discover their secrets. Borrow those ideas that will work for you.

Breakthrough! Have your departments and teams evaluate the quality of service they receive from each other. Survey their opinions about matters such as: (1) making needs and expectations clear, (2) reasonableness of requests, (3) quick response to requests, (4) treating other employees with respect, (5) providing timely and accurate information, (6) being collaborative not competitive, (7) having knowledgeable employees, (8) commitment to excellence and total quality, (9) acting consistent with corporate core values, (10) fulfilling promises and following through on commitments, (11) being open to criticism, (12) dealing effectively with change, and (13) taking a problem-solving approach to inter-team disputes. Analyze the results of the surveys and insist that the teams rated in the bottom 50% in the company submit an approved plan for moving up into the top half of the field.

And if the blind leads the blind, both will fall into a ditch.

~Matthew 15:14b

How can we equip our emerging leaders?

One-Minute Answer: Organizations that promote from within for high-level leadership send an encouraging message that dedication and good performance are rewarded. They also illuminate career paths for employees who want to know where hard work leads them. Promoting from the ranks puts teeth into succession planning.

The biblical wisdom about the difficulty of being a prophet in your own town explains why organizations sometimes reach beyond their borders for fresh leadership. The sense that there is someone better and brighter out there suggests that an external search, particularly for C-level executives, will generate more attractive resumes.

Either management selection approach can be effective. A recent study, however, found that over 60% of the C-level executives recruited from the outside fail within two years, while just over 40% of those promoted are likewise regretted in the same period. The primary reason for failures from without is a mismatch with the culture of the organization and an inability to make the necessary behavioral adjustments to achieve fit. The number one contributor to the collapse of internal candidates is the assumption that achievement at lower levels of responsibility automatically translates into triumph at more demanding levels of authority.

Are you an emerging leader who wants to be seen as worthy for the next level of responsibility? Or, are you responsible for grooming emerging leaders? Either way you'll want to read ahead.

Five-Minute Answer: The Executive Leadership Academy (TELA) elevates the success rate of leadership apprentices. Will this approach make sense for you personally as a higher-level hopeful, and will it work in your organization for the next generation of leaders?

TELA draws on the development tools described below. The best design for you depends on the mission, vision, values, beliefs, and culture of your organization as well as the experience and skill levels of apprentice leaders. The typical duration is 12 to 18 months.

1. **Identification.** Apprentices are nominated by their managers. The best candidates are those with limited experience at supervising people, but with great executive potential.

2. **Assessment.** At the outset, TELA apprentices receive 360° feedback on the reactions of others to their leadership to date. Based on this feedback the apprentice and an assigned professional coach map out a focused development plan for matriculation through the program. Specifically, each apprentice commits to three priority areas of improvement.

3. **Formative and Summative Evaluation.** The same 360° feedback tool is re-administered 50% of the way through TELA as feedback to the apprentice and coach. Another administration at the conclusion reveals the success of the experience for each apprentice, and perhaps the need for continued development.

4. **Coaching.** Assign coaches to apprentices based on results of the 360° assessment and the recommendations of their managers. Coaches play a key role in ensuring that participants grow in their ability to lead. Coaches check in with managers from time to time regarding the progress of the apprentices they nominated.

5. **Mentoring.** A mentor is chosen from the ranks of higher level executives outside the apprentice's direct chain of command. Mentors provide a listening ear and a perspective on what it takes to succeed within the corporate culture. Mentors and apprentices are trained together on how to gain most from the experience.

6. **Cohorts.** Apprentices experience the Academy in a cohort of peers. These cohorts—typically twelve—meet regularly to provide group support, responsibility, and perspective to members.

7. **Accountability Ally.** Apprentices select a partner from their cohort to encourage their progress and also to prod them to ensure follow-through on the commitments required by TELA.

8. **Emotional Competence Training.** The foundation of great leadership is high emotional competence. This training strengthens the interpersonal capability of participants. Its assessment nature provides a foundation for coaching.

9. **Leadership Training.** A leadership development course

containing 12-15 modules of instruction is spread out over the program in 90-minute sessions. This course is based on one taught at the Tepper School of Business at Carnegie Mellon University. Focused development beyond leadership can also be helpful in the areas of selling, customer service, presentation skills, conflict resolution, decision making, running effective meetings, handling media, and relationship building.

10. **"Ask Sam Deep."** Apprentices subscribe to Sam Deep's email blasts on leadership and personal effectiveness. Weekly topics provide great discussion with mentors, coaches, and cohorts.

11. **Business Cross-Training.** Apprentices rotate through the functional departments of the organization to increase their understanding of the total business, break down silos, and improve internal customer service. Especially crucial are HR policies and procedures and performance management systems.

12. **Cross-Generational Training.** Participants and their managers are sensitized to the sometimes contrasting views of life and work of emerging versus established leaders. This helps generations communicate well with each other, collaborate more fully, and learn from each other's strengths.

13. **In-Basket Simulations.** Apprentices receive simulation emails describing management challenges. They answer specific questions about how they will handle the challenges, receive feedback from their coaches and managers, and debate the solutions in subsequent cohort meetings.

14. **Culture Training.** Apprentices learn to incorporate the core values of the organization into their personal behavior and their leadership while empowering their teams and direct reports.

15. **Breakthrough Goal.** In addition to preparing participants for more challenging leadership responsibilities, TELA enables them to impact their current assignment. They establish a transformational objective to achieve during the second six months of the program. Members of their cohort, mentors, and coaches act as accountability partners.

Breakthrough! Write to sam@asksamdeep.com to learn how quickly and cost-effectively an Executive Leadership Academy can be established.

Man's chief purpose...is the creation and preservation of values; that is what gives meaning to our civilization, and the participation in this is what gives significance to the human life.

~Lewis Mumford

How can we create a positive company culture?

One-Minute Answer: There's much talk about corporate culture these days. So, what exactly is it? Culture is the way the people inside an organization relate to each other, to their work, and to their customers. The right culture translates into consistent prosperity, whether your corporate goals are for-profit or not-for-profit.

The leaders of a company make the effort to draw up a list of core values when they want to inculcate a particular culture. They hope these values will shape norms of behavior that collectively constitute an organizational way of life—one that leads to better outcomes.

Has your company established a powerful and a positive culture? Many make the effort to craft and transmit values to employees, but too few end up seeing those values directly and consistently influencing how employees actually behave.

What can you do to ensure that the values you select for your company inspire a culture that takes your organization to the next level of greatness?

Five-Minute Answer: Culture creation begins with the identification of values, but doesn't stop there. The real work is what you *do* with those values. How much of what's prescribed below has your company done? Have you been able to make it past #4?

1. **Ponder the universe of values.** Among these are accountability, character, creativity, dignity, excellence, honesty, integrity, leadership, personal responsibility, positive work ethic, respect, selflessness, stewardship, and teamwork.

2. **Don't confuse values with strategic priorities.** Values are attitudes and beliefs that compel behavior. The outcomes that you want those attitudes and beliefs to drive are *strategic priorities*, such as these: client focus, continuous improvement, corporate citizenship, cutting edge technology, developing people, diversity, employee engagement, health, innovation, safety, shareholder value, and sustainability. How well these

priorities are achieved is evidence of adherence to your values and ultimately to the strength of your culture.

3. **Identify your values.** Limit yourself to three or four values. The further you exceed three, the more your values will mirror everyone else's. Here's your chance to define a distinctive corporate culture to accomplish distinctive goals.

4. **Choose how you'll express them.** Once you succeed in distinguishing values from priorities, there are alternative ways of expressing them to employees, customers, and the rest of the world. One idea is to enumerate the specific behavioral expectations required within each value—an especially effective way to communicate fully the intent of the values to employees who are expected to live them. A second, less comprehensive approach is simply to attach a catch phrase to each one-word value. The four sample values below are now ready to undergird the strategic priorities you have also committed to.

Excellence	Respect	Integrity	Leadership
"Giving our best"	"Valuing each other"	"Doing the right thing"	"Showing the way"

5. **Preach them.** Let me tell you a story about CEO Stan—not his real name. At almost every meeting with the emerging leaders in his company he hands over $20 bills from his own wallet to those who can recite from memory selected portions of the mission, vision, and values of the firm. His actions convince managers that the values are important to him and therefore to them. A positive culture follows Stan everywhere he leads.

6. **Integrate them into hiring.** State your values in recruitment literature. Post them in advertising for new people. Use them to make hiring decisions by asking candidates to rank the company's values from most to least important and explain their choices. Or, press them to choose the one value they expect to fulfill most readily and one that they expect will be more challenging than the rest. Both exercises reveal a great deal about candidates while they stress the importance of values. (67-69)

7. **Integrate them into new employee orientation.** Here is another opportunity, not to be missed, to vaccinate the uninitiated with your company's belief system.

8. **Integrate them into special events.** Make clear to employees the connection between core values and community projects, charitable campaigns, and celebrations. Remind employees at every opportunity of why you do what you do beyond the workplace.

9. **Role model them.** Members of the leadership team, from first-line supervisor to CEO, must regularly challenge each other on how well their individual and collective behavior reflect what they profess to be important. How well do they walk the talk?

10. **Integrate them into training and development.** Make every training session and development program in your company internally consistent with your values. Actually teach courses on how to integrate them into the workplace.

11. **Integrate them into performance management.** Make sure your employee goal-setting form contains a section where employees are pressed to commit to greater integration of core values and individual performance. Also, the portion of your performance review that assesses behavior, as opposed to measurable outcomes, should focus specifically on adherence to your core values. And, employees placed on performance improvement plans typically have the need to improve relative to one or more of the core values. Be certain the plan specifies that. (63-65)

12. **Provide consequences.** Reward compliance with, and discipline defiance toward, core values. Nothing convinces employees more that you mean business.

Breakthrough! Seize every opportunity to evaluate culture. Conduct employee job satisfaction surveys. Perform customer service satisfaction assessments. Hire mystery shoppers. Examine the overall evaluations employees receive on the *how* side of performance reviews. Get upward feedback for managers on how well they live the values. At exit interviews learn what voluntarily and involuntarily terminated employees think of the culture. Make the improvements that these and other culture evaluations cry for.

There are no bad customers; only those who are harder to please than others.

~Said by someone who's never waited on a customer in his or her life!

How do I get my employees to provide world-class service?

One-Minute Answer: I once consulted to a large company in the health care supply business where the CEO regularly reminded his employees about "King Customer".

He took advantage of every possible communication opportunity with employees, with his board of directors, and with anyone who would listen to his customer-centric creed. At the time I thought, "What better cause to focus employees on is there than customers?" But, as employees felt increasingly willing to be open with me, they revealed their reactions to the "King Customer" mantra. As one manager put it, "Yeah, the customer is king...and that means we're slaves!" As it turned out, the CEO, was a "just do it" leader who believed he could cajole his employees into customer service excellence.

Several years ago Hal Rosenbluth of Rosenbluth Travel wrote a book with the intriguing title, *The Customer Comes Second*. Get it? It's your employees, not your customers, who are kings. Treat them like royalty and they'll return the favor to you in many forms—not the least of which will be the attention they give to the people who use your products and services.

If you come to me with a budget of $250,000 to improve the quality of service (please do!), I'll suggest we spend $200,000 to improve the leadership your service providers receive and only $50,000 to teach your people the stuff you'll find below. Yet it's really good! (3-13)

Five-Minute Answer: In the 1980's American businesses were outdistanced by those from other nations—particularly Japan—and customer service was recognized as a major route back to success. One organization that came to the fore to help address our economic woes was the International Customer Service Association (ICSA). I had the opportunity to speak to its members on three different occasions.

Here's the content from one of my ICSA talks:

Eight Commandments of Exceptional Customer Service

1. **Build personal relationships.** You want customers to feel so

good about you that three things happen: (1) they keep coming back without you having to re-sell them, (2) when you do have to resell them you have a distinct edge over the competition, and (3) when you mess up they'll cut you colossal slack. One way to bond with clients is to listen to them with such sincerity that they're willing to tell you important stuff about themselves and thereby build intimacy in the relationship. Another connector is to thank them and to give them credit for the things they do to make it easier for you to serve them. (55-57)

2. **Reveal your value proposition.** Tell your customers (and by extension, your employees) exactly what they can expect your service to look like and more importantly what outcomes they can expect to derive from that service. Here's a great value proposition one of my clients lived by:

> We pledge to our customers that we will...
> - ☐ Exceed your expectations of us
> - ☐ Ensure your success through the distribution of our products and services
> - ☐ Work with you to meet your challenges and accomplish mutual goals
> - ☐ Serve you with unquestionable integrity
> - ☐ Treat your employees with the utmost respect

3. **Say what you need from them.** Expectations never go in only one direction. Have you told your customers what you need from them in order for you to give what you've pledged to them? You may be surprised to learn how willing they are to help you help them.

4. **Serve them!** Customers shouldn't have to ask more than once for what they want. Anticipate their needs so well that you provide it for them even before they ask. Nor should they have to lift a finger to get quality service. You make the call, fill out the form, "walk" them to where they need to be, smooth over their mistakes, and go the extra mile. They are not in business to make your job easier; it's the other way around.

5. **Affirm them.** All customers should leave your presence feeling that they are important to you and to your company. They'll believe this, or not, depending on the tone of voice you have

used in your conversation with them. Is it warm, understanding, and supportive? Your words are equally important. Do you say "hello" rather than "hi"; "May I help you?" rather than "Can…?" and "My pleasure" rather than "No problem"? Your body language counts as well. Do you look at your customers with smiling eyes?

6. **Provide solutions, not service.** You've not done your job once you've done your job. An oxymoron? No! As an executive coach, it's tempting for me to think I've met the terms of my contract with a leader once we've analyzed and acted on all the assessments we've agreed to and once we've had all the coaching sessions on the docket. But the bottom line is that I haven't served the executive until he or she has become a more effective leader. In the same way, your employees need to know that "I did what the customer wanted" is no substitute for "The customer is thrilled by what I did."

7. **Head off betrayal.** President Ronald Reagan commissioned a study on the state of customer service in America. One of the outcomes of that study revealed that for every 27 dissatisfactions a company might cause its customers only one of those returns to the company as a voiced complaint. Furthermore, each of the dissatisfied, but silent customers is likely to badmouth you to another ten people who will relay that displeasure to another five. And ultimately 90% of them will stop doing business with you. What can we take away from this finding? We don't hear enough complaints! So how do we get them? Start conducting regular customer service satisfaction assessments of your ongoing clients. Learn what they really think of you.

8. **Make it right quickly, happily, remorsefully, generously, and thankfully.** General George S. Patton once said, "I don't measure a man by how high he can climb, but by what he does after he falls down." In that vein, I'm not looking for service providers in my life who always get it right the first time. That's not possible. But I *am* looking for a determination to get it right the *second* time. (91-93)

Breakthrough! Look back to #7 above. Learn to ask your customers "one-finger" questions. Stop asking, "How are we doing?" which almost always elicits a dutiful "fine". Instead, put the word "one" somewhere in your request for customer feedback. My personal favorite is, "What's the *one* thing we could do to lose your business?"

*Anger as soon as fed is dead—
'Tis starving makes it fat.*

~Emily Dickinson

What should we do about angry customers?

One-Minute Answer: In 1992, I co-authored *What to Say to Get What You Want: Strong Words for 44 Challenging Bosses, Employees, Coworkers, and Customers.* While complaining customers headlined their section of the book, eight other challenging types joined them. The full cast of characters looked like this:

Complainers are upset by something they believe you did or failed to do.

VIPs demand special treatment, owing to their sense of entitlement.

Deceivers try to hoodwink you for personal gain.

Negotiators are first cousins to Deceivers and VIPs in that they're continually pushing for a better deal.

Sponges are the 20% of your customers who consume 80% of your time and perhaps your resources.

Non-Compliants fail to read instructions, pay attention to signs, and otherwise refuse to meet your needs for behavior that enables you to serve them well.

Destroyers in retail situations damage displays and products or leave a mess in their wake.

Loudmouths are loud, rude, profane, insulting, or physically confrontive.

Derelict Guardians allow their kids to be Destroyers or Loudmouths.

The bosses, employees, coworkers, and customers that we wrote about in that book were pretty ornery. You and your employees are about to learn how to handle just one of the customers—the *Complainer.* That's the bad news. The good news is that much of the guidance below is helpful with the VIP, Deceiver, Loudmouth, and Negotiator as well as the rest. And even many of the 35 unmentioned bosses, employees, and coworkers from the book will be managed better with these approaches.

Five-Minute Answer: Here's the best possible sequence for transforming an angry customer into one eager to give you a second chance to get it right. These ten tips are taken from my workshop: "Quality Service: Defining It, Building It, and Sustaining It."

1. **Listen.** Your ears will immediately start winning over customers who feel betrayed. When the confrontation is in person you'll be aided by slightly elevated eyebrows, a half smile, and an occasional nod. Your aims are, first, to allow the person to vent and calm down and, second, to learn as many facts as you can about what happened. Offer no solutions until *both* of these goals have been achieved. (39-41)

2. **Remain calm.** If you deal directly with customers, there's an item in your job description that you may have overlooked: "Encounters three buyer beatings a day." Anticipation prepares you to deal with rancorous customer complaints. It gives you the presence of mind that brings angry customers down to your level of emotionality rather than you rising to theirs.

3. **Validate the customer.** A number of years ago I consulted to the customer service team of a manufacturer and distributor of high tech medical devices. This was one of the many consulting assignments where I learned as much as I taught. In this case, my education came from the service manager who dispatched technicians to hospitals to resolve equipment failures. His sendoff still resonates with me: "Fix the customer before you fix the equipment." He knew that a compassionate statement such as, "This shouldn't have happened to you" was as important as making sure it didn't happen again.

4. **Ask questions.** You may not have to ask questions to get the Complainer to vent fully (see #1), but you will almost certainly have to probe for additional data you need to determine what your corrective action, if any, should be. But do not attempt this until you have calmed the customer.

5. **Prove you listened.** When others tell you something, either on their own or after you've asked a question, they'll look for evidence that you listened. So, give it to them! Reflect or paraphrase their assertions. A favorite of mine is, "Did I hear correctly that you...?" Nothing beats action, but "At least they listened to me" isn't a bad thing to have working for you in second place.

6. **Apologize and ask to make it right.** I learned of Jack Paar's "We Care" customer service program when he and I provided national training for Hallmark Cards store owners. Boy, can he teach on this point! You should hear the sincerity and compassion in Jack's voice when he says, "I'm so sorry this happened to you. Will you forgive us, and are you willing to give us the opportunity to make it right for you?"

7. **Be politely assertive with unreason.** Peek back at the description above of VIPs, Deceivers, and Negotiators. Imagine what those customers are going to insist that you do to solve their problems! Prepare, first, to matter-of-factly handle untruths they may fabricate: "Actually, our contract makes that stipulation. You may have missed it in Article VI, Section 3." Prepare, second, to insist on a reasonable solution without unnecessarily saying "no" when they push the envelope: "Let me tell you what we *can* do."

8. **Thank the customer.** "I appreciate the opportunity you've given us to correct the problem you brought to our attention."

9. **Take action.** Make it right as quickly and as generously as you can. The Red Robin Restaurant chain won my loyalty by how they handled a failure to include "Red's Rice Bowl" special sauce in a takeout order. I didn't discover the oversight until I got home and then had to concoct a substitute sauce with kitchen ingredients and the advice of the employee I phoned. Even better was the $20 Red Robin gift card I received in the mail a few days later.

10. **Check back.** Is the customer happy with your corrective action? Find out, but please don't make your request for feedback as intrusive as some of the on-line surveys I'm asked to complete following support from a help desk. Ask a simple question: "Did we make it right for you, and if not what will it take?"

Breakthrough! Use these ten points to create the curriculum for an employee workshop on handling complaining customers. Provide opportunity in the class for students to role play their responses to the typical complaints that your employees receive.

Satisfaction guaranteed or double your garbage back.

~Sign on garbage truck
in Cambridge, Massachusetts

What wisdom is out there about serving customers?

One-Minute Answer: There are four ways to beat the competition. Offer a lower price, produce a better product, deliver it quicker, or make it easier and more enjoyable for customers to deal with you. That means that with the sole exception of pricing, service plays a major role in winning customer loyalty.

Try as we might, it's often futile to preach to employees on the urgency of serving customers. A lecture, an exhortation, or a scolding may light fires *under* them, but won't ignite passions *within* them.

So how can you turn them on to their jobs? How can you kindle an internal flame that transforms them into spirited and willing servants of the people who buy your products and services?

Five-Minute Answer: Here is a collection of sayings assembled just for you. Memorize one or two to quote at the right time to encourage behavior you're looking for. Post them over time in a place for all to see and be uplifted by. Or, insert them into customer service training course materials.

The Heart of Customer Service

"Customers pay only for what is of use to them and gives them value. Nothing else constitutes quality."
~Peter Drucker

"Consumers are statistics. Customers are people." *~Stanley Marcus*

"From our customers' point of view, if they can see it, walk on it, hold it, hear it, step in it, smell it, carry it, step over it, touch it, use it, even taste it, if they can feel it or sense it, it's customer service."
~SuperAmerica (gasoline and food chain)

"The best customer to have is the one you've already got."
~Dick Shaaf

The Positive Impact of Satisfying Customers

"He profits most who serves best." *~Arthur F. Sheldon*

"Treat people as if they were what they ought to be and you help them to become what they are capable of being."

~Johann Wolfgang von Goethe

"There are painters who transform the sun to a yellow spot, but there are others who with the help of their art and their intelligence, transform a yellow spot into the sun." *~Pablo Picasso*

"It is not the employer who pays the wages. Employers only handle the money. It is the customer who pays the wages." *~Henry Ford*

Challenges for Customer Servers

"People who really want help may attack you if you help them. Help them anyway." *~Mother Teresa*

"People seldom refuse help, if one offers it in the right way."

~A. C.Benson

"One must really have suffered oneself to help others."

~Mother Teresa

"Tell others of the positive effects of their actions. It will help return the kindness they showed to you." *~Dan Kelly*

"Great opportunities to help others seldom come, but small ones surround us every day." *~Sally Koch*

"Your most unhappy customers are your greatest source of learning."

~Bill Gates

Positive Outcomes for Customer Servers

"The sole meaning of life is to serve humanity." *~Leo Tolstoy*

"You can't help someone get up a hill without getting closer to the top yourself." *~General H. Norman Schwarzkopf*

"Sure I'm helping the elderly. I'm going to be old myself some day."

~Lillian Carter

"Little deeds of kindness, little words of love, help to make earth happy like the heaven above." *~Julia A. Fletcher Carney*

"The more credit you give away, the more it will come back to you. The more you help others, the more they will want to help you."

~Brian Tracy

"Find a job you like and you add five days to every weekend."
~H. Jackson Brown, Jr.

Corporate Slogans about Commitment to Customers

"We'll go to the ends of the earth for you."   ~Continental Airlines

"When it absolutely, positively has to be there overnight."   ~Fedex

"Have it your way."   ~Burger King

"We do it all for you."   ~McDonalds

"So easy a caveman can do it."   ~GEICO

Breakthrough! Lead a lunch 'n learn for your employees with these quotes posted on the walls. Ask them to choose four of the quotes according to these criteria: (1) one that most characterizes the attention your company's customers receive, (2) one that least characterizes that service, (3) their personal favorite from the list, and (4) the one they personally find most challenging to model with customers. Encourage a discussion of everyone's choices.

A boss is someone who's early when you're late and late when you're early.

~Unknown author

How can I build credibility with my boss?

One-Minute Answer: The CEO who commands the respect of her Board is free to lead with confidence. The VP who pleases his CEO will become a succession candidate. The manager prized by the VP she reports to is going places. The administrative assistant who wins the favor of his manager has job security and career potential.

Your success is determined more than anything else by the person you report to. You need that person's backing when you go up against others. You need that person's assent for your ideas. You need that person's honest feedback on your performance. You need that person's grace for your mistakes. You need that person's vote when the next promotion opportunity arrives.

Most people assume that the best way to get ahead is to do good work and therefore be seen as a rising star. Not a bad assumption, but an incomplete one. Several of the high-performing executives I've coached were among the best-kept secrets in their companies because they neglected a core duty. They failed to be in service to the person they reported to. They failed to build sufficient credibility with their boss.

Are you certain that you're performing that duty? Are you a prized follower? It may be worth five minutes to take a test and find out.

Five-Minute Answer: The assessment below is in four parts. Each one covers a different credibility-building component of your relationship with the person you report to. Get the most out of each part by choosing the one behavior in that section that you display *more* fully (⇧) than the others and the one that you display *less* fully (⇩) than the others.

Part A: Understanding My Boss (circle one ⇧ and one ⇩)

1.   ⇧   ⇩   I know my boss's vision, dreams, values, beliefs, aspirations, and need—what's really important to him or her.

2.   ⇧   ⇩   I know the expectations my boss has for my

performance—how he or she wants me to carry out my duties.

3. ⇧ ⇩   I pin my boss down for critical details regarding assigned projects when those success factors aren't made clear up front.

4. ⇧ ⇩   I am able to see issues through my boss's eyes; I accurately anticipate his or her every reaction.

5. ⇧ ⇩   I know what he or she considers my strengths and weaknesses to be and in what areas I'm expected to improve.

Part B: Problem Solving and Initiating (circle one ⇧ and one ⇩)

6. ⇧ ⇩   I recommend alternative solutions for the problems I bring to his or her attention.

7. ⇧ ⇩   I suggest ways to reduce expenses or to spend money more efficiently.

8. ⇧ ⇩   I suggest ways to increase revenue, find new markets, or do a better job of delighting customers.

9. ⇧ ⇩   I recommend ways to do things better and faster; I'm a fountain of ideas for continuous improvement.

10. ⇧ ⇩   I stretch beyond my job description, hunting down solutions to problems that I may not necessarily be expected to solve; I take initiative.

11. ⇧ ⇩   I welcome new challenges and responsibilities.

Part C: Communicating (circle one ⇧ and one ⇩)

12. ⇧ ⇩   I keep my boss well informed of my progress on projects he or she needs to keep track of.

13. ⇧ ⇩   I give my coworkers, particularly those who also report to my boss, the information they need from me to perform their jobs successfully.

14. ⇧ ⇩   I communicate to my boss with positive, can-do language.

15. ⇧ ⇩   My language skills are sharp; I am an accurate communicator.

16. ⇧ ⇩   My boss approves/adopts a majority of the ideas I
           suggest.

17. ⇧ ⇩   I speak and act respectfully toward my boss and behind
           his or her back.

Part D: Performing (circle one ⇧ and one ⇩)

18. ⇧ ⇩   I am reliable and consistent; I can be counted on to
           deliver and to follow through.

19. ⇧ ⇩   My word is my bond to my boss, my colleagues, and my
           customers; I am honest.

20. ⇧ ⇩   I treat both internal and external customers in a way
           that reflects positively on my boss.

21. ⇧ ⇩   I accept full responsibility for the outcomes of my
           efforts.

22. ⇧ ⇩   I am open to feedback on my performance from my
           boss; I accept it and use it to improve the quality of my
           work.

23. ⇧ ⇩   I succeed at making my boss's job easier and reducing
           the pain in his or her work life.

Breakthrough! Are you serious about maximizing the respect your
boss has for you? If so, copy this assessment with your four upward
and downward arrows circled. Present it to your boss with a request
that the two of you discuss your choices at a meeting a week later.
If you're not serious enough to take such a step, find someone
else in a position to give you feedback on your arrows. If you're
even less serious than that, do two things: First, celebrate your
four ⇧'s—you've earned a pat on the back, even if it has to be self-
administered. Second, make a vow to yourself that you'll improve
your behavior on your four ⇩'s.

To see your drama clearly is to be liberated from it.

~Ken S. Keyes, Jr.

What are some awful ways to be seen by my boss?

One-Minute Answer: On pages 99 to 101 you learned how to build credibility with your boss. That counsel pointed you to what supervisors, executives, and boards of directors look for in their direct reports.

You may be equally interested to know what *upsets* the people you report to. Since the behaviors that bosses find troubling go beyond being opposite the earlier advice, you might not readily guess what they are.

You would think that most bosses are forthcoming with their feedback on what annoys them. Not so! The famed Edwards Deming—father of the total quality movement—hypothesized that 80% of American managers have little idea of how they are seen by their bosses.

So I'll take the bull by the horns and give you a list of the most frequent character and behavior traits that managers tell me bug them. Then it'll be up to you to do an insightful self-assessment.

Bulletin! The information that follows is equally instrumental for bosses who seek to modify the problematic behavior of those in their employ.

Five-Minute Answer: Here's some bad news: there are twenty distinctive followers that pain bosses. Here's the good news: this is an opportunity to find out if you are a source of such pain and to take steps to remove it without having to remove yourself.

In each case the troublesome employee has a name, utters a typical comment, and reveals expected behavior.

20 Disturbing Direct Reports

Name	Typical Comment	Expected Behavior
Can-Do	"No problem—I'll get on it right away!"	Seldom keeps promises; volunteers for tasks rarely done and deadlines not met
Deaf Ear	"I don't remember you saying that."	Ignores directions; listens selectively; what he has to say is what's most important
Defeatist	"Let me explain why that won't work."	Pessimist; sees the downside; fears risk; pushes back on proposed actions before asked
Denier	"I did everything expected of me."	Can't express regret; shirks responsibility for outcomes or how those outcomes affect others
Empire Builder	"That function needs to be in my area."	Looks to build preeminence and importance by increasing the scope of her responsibilities
Fountain	"...and that reminds me to say this.."	Talks too much; circumvents issues; takes too long to get to the point; bloviates
Historian	"We tried that before."	Clings to earlier times; fiercely protects tradition; resists change; blames the past
Insubordiate	"Why must I be the one to change?"	Fails either to submit to authority or get a new job—the two best choices; may sabotage higher ups
Know-It-All	"Yes, but here's another way to..."	Takes advantage of every opportunity to have the last word and demonstrate how smart he is
Self-Promoter	"What's in it for me?"	Sense of entitlement; takes more than she gives; convinced she deserves better

Sharp Tongue	"You have a lot to learn."	Adds two cents; passes judgement; makes destructive comments; sarcastic
Shirker	"I'm the hardest worker in the office."	Not carrying his share of the load; disappears when work intensifies; takes lots of time off
Short Fuse	"I've *had* it."	Speaks in anger; emotionally volatile and disruptive; gets highly defensive at feedback
Showboat	"I was the one who made that happen."	Takes credit even when not due; is absent humility; bathes in praise; needs to be the star
Subversive	"I'm only doing what's best."	Feels justified in her attempts to bring others down; may scheme to take over someone's position
Sycophant	"Boss, we're so lucky to have you."	Praises higher ups effusively; won't bring bad news; waits for boss to commit so he can agree
Whiner	"It could have been so much better."	Gripes, grouses, and complains; speaks in negative terms even about positive outcomes
Wimp	"Let's not take needless chances."	Plays close to the vest; takes sure path; risk averse; failure preventer not success insurer
Withholder	"I assumed you didn't need to know that."	Fails to keep others informed; oblivious to the needs others have for accurate, timely updates
Underachiever	"Nobody's perfect."	Not living up to her potential; not striving to get better

Breakthrough! Regarding your boss, give the list to him or her for feedback. For each of the score of scourges request a green light (not at all you), yellow light (sometimes you), or red light (too often you). This may sound scary, but it's certain to be of benefit. Regarding your direct reports, meet with each one of them and go through the same green, yellow, and red light ratings. Add recommendations for steps they can take to turn red and yellow lights into greens.

He that cannot obey cannot command.

~Benjamin Franklin

What wisdom is out there about serving bosses?

One-Minute Answer: Before you can reach your fullest potential as a leader you must become the best possible follower.

Three things are needed. First, plant in your head what it means to serve others in positions of authority—understand what leadership really is. Second, send that knowledge to your heart so you desire to serve with distinction—want to be the best leader possible. Third, let your heart activate your hands, mouth, and feet to demonstrate that fervor.

Learn how to take these three "followership" steps toward great leadership by studying the insights of some very smart and experienced leaders.

Five-Minute Answer: Check out these stimulating statements *[and commentaries]* about pleasing the person you report to. Perhaps you will find one that inspires you to strengthen the relationship you have with the person you report to.

"Natural talent, intelligence, a wonderful education—none of these guarantees success. Something else is needed: the sensitivity to understand what other people want and the willingness to give it to them." ~*John Luther*

[Great followers discover what their leaders want and then deliver. It's that simple.]

"You can't make the other fellow feel important in your presence if you secretly feel that he is a nobody." ~*Les Giblin*

[You'll not hide disrespect that may be in your heart for those in authority. It will be revealed uncontrollably by tone of voice and body language. Your only choice is to change your heart—or change your job.]

"There is a rule in sailing that the more maneuverable ship should give way to the less maneuverable craft. I think this is sometimes a good rule to follow in human relationships as well."

~*Dr. Joyce Brothers*

[Most bosses want your ideas, but when they've listened and made it clear they've heard enough, it's time to back down—even when you "know" you're right.]

"If you would have a happy life, remember two things: In matters of principle, stand like a rock; in matters of taste, swim with the current."   ~Thomas Jefferson

[Choose your fights well. The more often you disagree the less impact your positions will have. Be certain your resistance and advocacy are truly meaningful to the organization, to customers, and to you.]

"If you are suffering from a bad man's injustice, forgive him lest there be two bad men."   ~Augustine

[Don't you wish people would get what they deserve? Aren't you glad you don't? Forgive; it frees you.]

"When I'm getting ready to persuade a man, I spend one-third of my time thinking about myself and what I'm going to say and two-thirds thinking about him and what he's going to say."   ~Abraham Lincoln

[Sell ideas based on benefits that appeal to your boss—not you or others.]

"It's when you rub elbows with a man that you find out what he has up his sleeve."   ~Unknown author

[It's quite impossible to serve leaders well without knowing them well enough to understand their vision—their dissatisfaction with the present, and desire to create a new tomorrow. What future does your boss strive for?]

"A wise man associating with the vicious becomes an idiot; a dog traveling with good men becomes a rational being."   ~Arabic proverb

[Once there is no longer any question that you report to an evil person, leave.]

"Don't drown the man who taught you to swim."   ~C. H. Spurgeon

[Continue honoring people for what you have learned from them, even when they become unhelpful leaders. And never go over a boss's head. Yours is not likely to be the rare case where it pays off for anyone.]

"To be humble to superiors is duty; to equals is courtesy; to inferiors, nobleness."   ~Benjamin Franklin

[Each of these three behaviors reinforces the other. Treat any of these groups with less than respect and the other two will likely suffer under your hand.]

"Think of three things: whence you came, where you are going, and to whom you must account."   ~Benjamin Franklin

[I sometimes ask executives to rate how well their direct reports show accountability for the results of their work. When I let them use a rating scale of 0 to 10, the average score given is about a 7. What number does your boss give you?]

"Everyone must submit himself to the governing authorities, for there is no authority except that which God has established. The authorities that exist have been established by God. Consequently, he who rebels against the authority is rebelling against what God has instituted, and those who do so will bring judgment on themselves. For rulers hold no terror for those who do right, but for those who do wrong. Do you want to be free from fear of the one in authority? Then do what is right and he will commend you. For he is God's servant to do you good. But if you do wrong, be afraid, for he does not bear the sword for nothing. He is God's servant, an agent of wrath to bring punishment on the wrongdoer. Therefore, it is necessary to submit to the authorities, not only because of possible punishment but also because of conscience."   ~Rom 13:1-5 (NIV)

[This reading comes up often in discussions with clients who struggle with allegiance to a boss they believe is mismanaging them. It tells me that they need to either quit or submit—either invariably leads to freedom. Perhaps another implication is that even bad bosses are there for a reason. It may be something you need to learn about yourself.]

Breakthrough! Do any of the quotes plus commentary above make you uncomfortable or even trigger disagreement? That is very likely the attitude and behavior that is most urgent for you to improve!

How Can Sam Deep Help Me?

Sam Deep fulfills one or more of these roles with his clients:

Executive Advisor and Coach. The top positions in an organization can be lonely places. I may be the right person to help you discover, according to Pareto, the 20% of your day that creates 80% of your leadership impact.

Team Builder. Teams at the top often require greater unity and a common cause. Occasionally, broken relationships are in need of healing, and are duplicated down through the ranks. We can increase teamwork, break down silos, resolve interpersonal conflict, and improve internal customer service.

Leadership Developer and Trainer. For eight years I taught "Meeting the Challenges of Corporate Leadership" to 2nd year MBA's in the Tepper School of Business at Carnegie Mellon University. Coming from that experience the *Leadership Academy* will be tailored to your emerging, high-potential, succession leadership candidates.

Motivational Speaker. You may want me to kick off or conclude your next management conference with a presentation on one of over 20 topics in leadership, communication, team building, and personal achievement. Each talk will feature the blend of humor, inspiration, and substance that you require.

Presentation Skills Coach. Do your executives need to improve their ability to stand up and deliver at conferences, board meetings, sales presentations, or instructional settings? From my training, videotaping, and feedback they'll make dramatic improvements.

Performance Management Advisor. Many of my clients welcome help creating performance review processes that for the first time actually improve performance.

Process Consultant. You and I will implement a strategic planning vehicle that is sensitive to where you are and takes you where you need to go. Or we may choose to apply the powerful "retrospective thinking" exercise to an upcoming crisis, opportunity, or major change. Other solutions are fully tailored to the problems you face.

Take the next step by calling (412) 487-2379 or emailing sam@asksamdeep.com.